The Life of Cardinal Reginald Pole
by Lodovico Beccadelli

Copyright © 2019 by HardPress

Address:
HardPress
8345 NW 66TH ST #2561
MIAMI FL 33166-2626
USA
Email: info@hardpress.net

Biogr. 905 *ld*

Becc.

Bayer. Staatsbibliothek

THE LIFE OF Cardinal Reginald Pole,

Written originally in ITALIAN,

BY

Lodovico Beccatelli,

Archbishop of RAGUSA;

And now first translated into ENGLISH.

With NOTES Critical and Historical.

To which is added,

An APPENDIX,

Setting forth

The Plagiarisms, False Translations, and False Grammar in THOMAS PHILLIPS's History of the Life of REGINALD POLE.

By the Reverend BENJAMIN PYE, LL.B.

Usu sæpe venit, ut qui, toto orationis apparatu concinnè atque copiosè constructo, coacervandis texendisque laudibus tantum student, dum consulto præterire quicquam nollent eorum quæ ad EUM de quo scribunt amplificandum faciunt, ommittent tamen nonnunquam VERITATEM; *tum nimiæ laudis studio provecti, factis criminationibus lacessent eos quos adversos senserint;—Id quod* POLO *celebrando* ITALIS ORATORIBUS *commune semper fuit.*

PARKER de Antiquitate Ecclesiæ Britannicæ, p. 514.

LONDON, Printed;
And Sold by C. BATHURST, in Fleet-Street.
M.DCC.LXVI.

Bayerische
Staatsbibliothek
München

To the HONOURABLE
And RIGHT REVEREND

RICHARD,

LORD BISHOP of

DURHAM.

MY LORD!

I HAVE the honour of presenting to your LORDSHIP a faithful, tho' inelegant copy of a very ancient portrait of CARDINAL POLE, which by the flatterers of his memory is esteemed as an original of great value, although the *Italian Artist* who drew it seems to have been too lavish of his colouring, and too ambitious of presenting us with a pleasing, and high-finished piece, to have been sufficiently attentive to the justness of the resemblance.

These curious remains, my Lord, were lately rescued from the oblivion of almost two hundred years, by one of POLE's zealous admirers, Cardinal QUIRINI, who professes to have drawn the first outlines of *his* character of POLE from this *Italian Master*, though he hath filled up the canvas afterwards with some strange daubing of his own, in which he hath since been followed by a very humble COPYIST in our own language.

It may not therefore, my Lord! be altogether unseasonable to exhibit a true and simple representation of the ORIGINAL itself; which, though modest in its appearance in comparison with the

DEDICATION.

the piece of a late biographer, hath too much of the fictitious cast of panegyric to have been offered to the public, unless it had been contrasted at the same time with the plainness and simplicity of historical truth, that it may be seen at one view, not only what POLE's transcendent merits were in the partial eye of his secretary and dependent BECCATELLI; but also what was his true and genuine character in his travels, his retirements, his embassies, his legation, and his primacy—

What are the virtues to be expected from men of high rank and distinguished accomplishments, when placed in the most exalted stations of the church, your LORDSHIP can best comprehend, who habitually practise them all with a grace and dignity peculiarly your own. Whether Cardinal POLE failed in such a disa display of them as became his character, we may easily discern, who have the model from which to judge of their true size and proportion.

His noble birth, and early taste for literary improvements, soon marked him out to his prince as the person on whom to bestow one of the first dignities in the church——yet he felt not those reciprocal obligations to loyalty and affection, which good and great minds have a stronger sense of, the nearer they approach to the person of their sovereign.

He had a polite knowlege of letters, and of mankind, and a commanding gracefulness of mien and manners——Yet, he employed not those engaging talents to win over the noble youth of his country to virtues worthy their emulation,

lation, by his address, and by his example; but ingloriously proftituted them in foreign kingdoms to the hoftile interefts of the avowed enemies of England.

His religion did not fhew itfelf by a ftrict guard over his own heart, and a mild and enlarged condefcenfion to the opinions of mankind—— but it allowed him (to the reproach of its tenets) to juftify difloyalty and rebellion in himfelf; and to tolerate unchriftian and unmanly feverities towards the perfons of others.

Such was the deftructive influence of bigotry and error on this exalted prelate, who in a better reign and under a happier guidance might have fhone forth one of the politeft noblemen, and accomplifhed churchmen of

DEDICATION.

Great Britain,—a character, which in its pure and unsullied lustre, may we long acknowlege and admire in the Bishop of Durham!

I am, my Lord,

    Your Lordship's

        Most Dutiful and

            Obedient Servant,

                  BENJAMIN PYE.

PREFACE.

A BIOGRAPHER seems to be by profession A WRITER OF PANEGYRIC; as it is a strong predilection in favour of some particular character, that generally determines him in the choice of his subject: Praise therefore being the fixed object of his plan, he often makes a sacrifice of truth without scruple, to his partiality for a friend, or his gratitude to a benefactor.

Compositions of this kind have therefore their principal merits in their elegant variety of compliment, and delicacy of expression; and it would be as unreasonable in a reader to complain of want of historical truth, in a work of pure declamation; as it would be absurd in a writer to make such effusions of the fancy,
however

however ingenious, the bafis and ground-work of real hiftory. The ITALIAN language, which, from its fmoothnefs and melody, is the very DIALECT of flattery, feems alfo peculiarly fuited to this fpecies of compofition; and the complexional genius of THAT nation, prone to admire every thing that is fpecious, together with the dependent State of the LITERATI among them, bred up either in the libraries of their popes, the palaces of their petty fovereigns, or the colleges of their cardinals, in the learned fervitude of librarians, and fecretaries, confpire to form the talents of their men of letters to this particular mode of writing.

This may be a probable reafon why writers of this clafs fhould be the more prodigal growth of ITALY than of any other foil; and they feem to have been at no period fo numerous as in the 16th CENTURY, when fcarce a perfon of eminence appeared among them but foon as ever he left the ftage, next to the marble buft, and monumental infcription, fucceeded the PANEGYRIC TO HIS MEMORY, though under the lefs flattering denomination of THE HISTORY OF HIS LIFE.

This

PREFACE.

This was the first essay * in which REGINALD POLE chose to try the strength of his pen at the age of TWENTY-FOUR, in which he hath paid a friendly, and at that time a very fashionable compliment, to a learned domestic.

His friends and cotemporary cardinals, CONTARINI, BEMBO, and SADOLET, all died before him, and were each of them celebrated by their several PANEGYRISTS, one of whom paid the same ingenious tribute afterwards to the memory of POLE himself.

BEMBO had his CASA, and SADOLET his FLOREBELLO; CONTARINI's LIFE and CHARACTER was probably the first effort of the grateful genius of his secretary BECCATELLI, who, if peradventure he hath shewn more elegance and agreeable variety in his HISTORICAL PANEGYRIC to the honour of the ENGLISH CARDINAL, may be supposed to owe

---

* VITA CHRISTOPHERI LONGOLII, prefixed to LONGOLIUS's Epistles; and published also in BATES's COLLECTION, intituled, VITÆ SELECTORUM ALIQUOT VIRORUM.

xii   PREFACE.

this improvement upon himself to his former succefsful trial in his LIFE OF CONTARINI †.

Both thefe pieces of BECCATELLI's were the employment of his learned retirement at his fee of RAGUSA, an employment not unbecoming of the moft exalted ftation.—The pleafing retrofpect of paft friendfhips! Neither did his ingenious gratitude die unremembered; the fame literary monument, which he had raifed to others, was afterwards erected to himfelf; and the benevolent archbifhop of RAGUSA had alfo his biographer *.

The life of my AUTHOR having never been publifhed, I fhall, in duty of his TRANSLATOR, felect a few anecdotes of his hiftory, fo far as concerns the prefent work, from his own writings, and other memoirs in the collections of C. QUIRINI.

---

† BECCATELLI's Life of Cardinal CONTARINI, written in ITALIAN, is publifhed in the 3d volume of C. QUIRINI's EPIST. R. POLI, printed at BRESCIA, 1748.

* Beccatelli Vita ab Antonio Gigante confcripta eft, & nondum typis edita.
                              Quirini, vol. i. p. 298.

He

PREFACE. xiii

He was a native of BOLOGNA, and being destined to a literary education, he went from thence to PADUA in the year 1528, to apply himself to the study of the GREEK language, which was the favourite ambition of every young student, and PADUA the most eminent school in which it was taught.

His studies were unhappily interrupted by the loss of his father, upon whose death he returned to BOLOGNA, where he commenced an acquaintance with COSMO GHERIO, bishop of FANO, who took him into his family, and carried him back again to PADUA, where he staid in the prosecution of his first plan, till the year 1532.

REGINALD POLE made his second visit to that university about this time, when they mutually engaged in a strict intimacy and friendship, which may be traced through the progress of both their lives for more than twenty succeeding years, till Cardinal Pole's promotion to the archbishoprick of CANTERBURY, and BECCATELLI's settlement in that of RAGUSA.

But this intimacy of theirs was not cemented by any particular connection till after the death of Cardinal CONTARINI in 1542, during which

which interval Beccatelli was HIS immediate secretary and domestic, and spent the seven last years in which that cardinal lived, chiefly in HIS family, who expired in his arms at BOLOGNA, August 24, 1542.

Upon this misfortune he seems to have passed over immediately into the houshold of C. POLE, carrying with him the grateful and affectionate remembrance of their common friend; and as he had oftentimes before been his companion and attendant in his journies and his embassies, he became now the chearful partner of his happier hours in his elegant retreat at VITERBO.

Here he indulged his natural bent to POETRY, the most delightful amusement of a disengaged mind, in the society of the gay and lively FLAMINIUS, who has addressed him in an ingenious copy of Verses published by Mr. POPE, in the second volume of the POEMATA ITALORUM: I have never seen any specimen of BECCATELLI's poetical talents, but we meet with a letter of complimental thanks to him, from his correspondent PRIULI, in return for TWO SONNETS he had sent to his friends in ENGLAND from RAGUSA, as late as the year 1556.

When

PREFACE. xv

When C. POLE was called away from his repose at VITERBO in 1545, BECCATELLI accompanied him, in character of secretary, to the council of TRENT: here we find him extremely busy in the duties of his office, and posting to and fro between Rome * and Trent, to receive fresh orders from the pope as new difficulties arose in the council, and to communicate to him MINUTES of all the business which passed there.

After this time he seems to have continued a domestic of the ENGLISH cardinal's; and it has been said (though not by BECCATELLI himself) was one among the vast shoal of ITALIANS who attended him into ENGLAND, to share in the bounty of a bigoted QUEEN, and in the pensions of a very opulent metropolitan: his stay, however, if he even was here, was very short, for we find him settled at RAGUSA, by a letter of Priuli's to him, in December 1556.

---

* C. Quirini, vol. iv. p. 277, & seq. Istruzzione per il nostro M. Lodovico Beccatelli, di quanto avrà da esporre a N. S. &c.

There

There is another letter on a more interesting subject written likewise in Italian, and addressed to him at the same place, in 1559, penned in a most melancholy strain by the same friend, upon the loss of their common patron CARDINAL POLE, whose death had so disordered Priuli's health, and affected his spirits, that he was not able to enter upon the tender office of imparting the news of it to BECCATELLI, till after an interval of many months.

Here too perhaps this very letter of PRIULI's might find him engaged in the affectionate task of compiling memoirs of the life and character of his former patron CONTARINI, when he was struck with the sad intelligence of the loss of another, and no less valued friend, Cardinal POLE; and the present bent of his thoughts and talents might incline him to vow the same offering to the memory of the English cardinal; which he probably executed the following year (as we may form some guess of the date of the Italian work by the publication of the Latin paraphrase of it by A. DUDITHIUS in less than three years afterwards).

One may suppose he was immediately urged to this undertaking at the request of PRIULI, who

who (as appears from a passage in the above letter) reserved the principal part of the cardinal's manuscripts as an intended present for BECCATELLI, which he proposed carrying with him to RAGUSA, as soon as his health and business would suffer him to leave ENGLAND.

I am not ignorant, that both PAULUS MANUTIUS and DUDITHIUS assert, that POLE's THEOLOGICAL works fell into the hands of cardinal MORONE who survived him; by whose means, those, and the rest of his MSS. came afterwards to be deposited in the VATICAN library, where cardinal Quirini found them about 20 years ago: but notwithstanding this, it is evident from the above letter, that it was the intention of POLE's executor PRIULI to have intrusted many of his papers, his MONUMENTI * DELL' INGEGNO, to the care of his

---

* Portando meco assai buona quantità delle reliquie, e MONUMENTI PRETIOSISSIMI DELL' INGEGNO, & della pietà, che ha lasciati questa santa anima.

    Aluise Priuli
     A Monsignor Lodovico Beccatelli,
Quirini, vol. v. p. 351. Ragusa.
      Di Londra, alla 13 di Giugno,
        1559.

     b   former

former secretary the archbishop of RAGUSA, who must have extracted from thence many anecdotes of his life.

I am not obliged, as his translator, to follow my author to his grave; the last that I know of him is, from FATHER PAUL, who introduces him as one of the speakers at the COUNCIL of TRENT in 1562.

His character, as Cardinal POLE's BIOGRAPHER, merits a little further examination, and will be best known from an unprejudiced discussion of the present work.

As a professed PANEGYRIST, he has dwelt upon, and embellished every incident of his story that can throw a lustre round his favourite character; and expunged, or cast into shades, whatever might seem to blemish or obscure it — And yet, notwithstanding this avowed partiality, either through a natural candour in his temper, or rather through a strong prepossession of the unblameableness of his hero's conduct, he has developed some * ac-

---

* Viz. The hostile intention of his two embassies—The pension he enjoyed from Charles V. &c.

tions

PREFACE.

tions of the Cardinal's life with a freedom and unreservedness uncommon in the writers of the papal party, which his copyists both in Latin and English, A. DUDITHIUS and T. PHILLIPS, have either diversified or disguised.

As a foreigner, he is very deficient in his knowlege of the history, customs, revenues, and even situation of our country; insomuch that I should apprehend (if no evidences appear to ascertain it) he never set his foot upon the island; but if he did, the very short stay he certainly made here, will intitle him to pardon for some not very material inaccuracies.

As a minute biographer, he has entered into a petty detail of every the most familiar circumstance of POLE's domestic œconomy and conversation: he has taken pains to bring us acquainted with his air, his person, and his countenance; and has even descended to a frivolous repetition of his table-talk, his sallies of mirth, and his repartees; which they, who can admire the like in PLUTARCH, may not disapprove in BECCATELLI.

Both the ITALIAN pieces of my author, by a particular fatality, have fallen into the hands of PLAGIARIES, who have mangled and disguised guifed them, and then, fent them abroad into the world as their own perfonal property.

J. CASA fet the example in the 16th century, in his Latin verfion of the life of cardinal CONTARINI; and he has been followed in the prefent by T. PHILLIPS, in his Englifh paraphrafe of the life of Cardinal POLE.

The former (as C. QUIRINI makes the obfervation) not only diffembles the character of a tranflator, but makes ufe of every artifice to evade the detection of his reader: the latter confeffes indeed, that fuch a perfon as BECCATELLI has trodden the path before him; but he fometimes tranflates him through a whole fection, without mentioning his name; and, when he does, it is with a tranfient acknowlegement for a fingle paragraph, when he is indebted to him perhaps for feveral pages.

BECCATELLI met with fomewhat more liberal treatment from ANDREAS DUDITHIUS, bifhop of KNYN in CROATIA, his friend, and, for a time, his affociate in Pole's family; who lived afterwards to retract his enthufiaftic admiration of the TRENTINE fynod, and muft of courfe have abated much of his veneration for HIM who had prefided in it: but fo great

was

PREFACE. xxi

was his attachment to the ENGLISH CARDINAL in the early part of his life, that he offered his service to BECCATELLI, to tranflate his Italian work into a more univerfal language; that the reputation of one he fo much admired, might not be circumfcribed within the boundaries of ITALY. This he executed afterwards, at the age of THIRTY, with the freedom and latitude of a PARAPHRAST, enlarged with many additional facts under the revifal of BAPTISTA BINARDI, who was POLE's fecretary after his fettlement in ENGLAND: which makes the latter part of POLE's life much more copious in the LATIN * verfion than in the ITALIAN original.

It were to be wifhed that DUDITHIUS would have prevailed with himfelf, at a maturer period of his life, to have revifed this work which he publifhed in 1563, when his more experienced knowlege of the inordinate luft of

---

* There are three editions extant of DUDITHIUS's Latin work:

One of Venice in 1563; one of LONDON in 1690; and another in 1696; to which may be added, that publifhed fince in the firft volume of Quirini's works, which PHILLIPS had before him, though he affects to refer to the Venetian edition of 1563.

power in the papal church, and his more settled judgment of the temper of HER advocates, would have greatly influenced the plan of his history, and have rendered it more complete and instructive——

He would then probably have pointed out to us the selfish motives ROME guided herself by, in the signal marks of her favour conferred on REGINALD POLE.

He would have acknowleged, that the INVECTIVE he wrote against HENRY VIII. was his first recommendation to the court of ROME: That PAUL III. raised him to the purple, to offer the greatest affront in his power to the king of ENGLAND: That he set him at the head of two successive councils to insult the crown of this realm in the person of an English subject; for as soon as HENRY was dead, POLE ceased to preside: That he employed him on embassies he was totally unequal to, that he might cast every imaginable indignity on the majesty of this kingdom.

And with regard to the CARDINAL himself; he would have allowed, that whatever had been the shining qualities of his earlier years; whatever might be the natural bent of his own

temper;

temper; yet his bigotted attachment to the CHURCH, and his implicit subjection to the COURT, of ROME, had absolutely incapacitated him, upon his recall to his country, from maintaining the character of the CANDID CHURCHMAN, or the ENGLISH NOBLEMAN.

What DUDITHIUS would have then written, had he revised this juvenile performance in praise of POLE, before he died in 1589, and what BECCATELLI must have acknowleged, had truth and not flattery been the object of his present performance, his translator has here endeavoured to display, by comparing the extravagant encomiums of POLE's implicit admirers, with the more faithful records of cotemporary writers.

Let this ELEGANT PIECE OF FLATTERY of BECCATELLI's have its true merits, and let it stand in the first rank of the many ingenious compositions of the same kind, which employed the pens of the literati in the 16th century; and let its characteristic title be, SPLENDIDE MENDAX.

But let not this sensible nation, ever intent on MANLY TRUTH, both in historical as well as philosophical inquiries, suffer * A WRITER to

* T. Phillips.

have

PREFACE.

have any share of credit or commendation here, whose boasted history is but THE SPURIOUS OFFSPRING OF A SPECIOUS PANEGYRIC.

NOTE:

The original work of BECCATELLI's, in Italian, is in the Vth volume of Cardinal QUIRINI's COLLECTIONS, intituled, " Epistolæ CARDINALIS POLI, & aliorum ad " ipsum,"—and was published from Two MSS. in the library at BRESCIA in 1757; one taken from the original MS. in the VATICAN at ROME, the other communicated to him by a family of the name of BECCATELLI, at BOLOGNA.

THE LIFE

OF

Cardinal Reginald Pole,

From the ITALIAN

OF

LODOVICO BECCATELLI.

THROUGH a motive of self-gratification, and in compliance with the request of many persons who have been earnest with me on this occasion, I propose writing the life of that eminent and illustrious Cardinal REGINALD POLE; in which I shall guide myself by the notices and observations which a friendship and familiarity of many years have enabled me to collect; having been myself an eye-witness of many events in his history, and indebted for other, either to his own information, or the testimony of those who were his chief friends and attendants during the principal transactions of his life, and at the time of his death: insomuch that

I flatter

I flatter myself I shall now exhibit, though wrought by the hand of a very unskilful artist, the picture of a man adorned with every virtue and excellence that are essential to the perfection of the true christian character; so large a portion of his bounty had the Divine Goodness been pleased to bestow upon him! And because these eminent qualities, I am now to speak of, were seated, and as it were enshrined in a most noble and princely extraction, I shall first give a short detail of the royal lineage of England, from one of whose most illustrious branches the Cardinal is descended.

THE Island of BRITAIN, now called ENGLAND, was anciently under the dominion of the BRITONS, and governed by her native kings, many of whom were of great renown, and, among the first, the illustrious ARTHUR, founder of the order of KNIGHTS OF THE ROUND TABLE, of whom both the historians and bards of that age speak with the highest honour. After his decease, by the cowardice and supineness of the succeeding kings, the BRITONS fell under the yoke of the ANGLES, a people of SAXONY, who divided the kingdom into several petty sovereignties, till EGBERT reduced them all under his own government, and became himself sole monarch of the island: this event was accomplished in the year 802.

THE BRITONS, thus driven from their ancient habitations, fled into other countries; part of them

them indeed still continued upon the island, retreating before their enemies into a mountainous quarter of it called WALES, where they have still kept their ground, and preserved their ancient language, which to this day is very different from that of the English, neither do the natives of each country easily understand one another. The Welsh in course of time became subject to the kings of England, yet the nobility of their nation were always esteemed of equal rank with the English nobles, and, as it is recorded in their annals, the illustrious house of ARTHUR, whose genealogy they trace with an exactness peculiar to their country, still exists in some of their principal families.

FROM this great ancestor they deduce the lineage of Henry VII. king of England, who possessed himself of the throne in the year 1486, to the great joy of the ENGLISH, who could ill brook the tyranny of RICHARD III. but still more of the WELSH, who now boasted, that the sovereignty was restored to the family of the illustrious Arthur [a]:

of

---

[a] Beccatelli has taken this whimsical genealogy of Sir Richard Pole, whom he makes to be a cousin of Henry VII. from some of the flattering writers of that king's reign, who, to discountenance the supposed obscurity of OWEN TUDOR's birth (cet homme inconnu qui n'avoit d'autre noblesse, ni d'autre titre que d'etre un homme bien fait—açcording to Mr. Hainault's account of him; Abregé chronologique, vol. 1.)

have

of the same lineage was Sir Richard Pole, the father of Reginald, being cousin to Henry VII. So that the Cardinal on his father's side was not only of very ancient and noble, but even of royal [b] descent. On his mother's side he was avowedly of royal birth, and very nearly related to the present race of kings. To explain this more fully, we must trace back the royal families of England for 250 years past, by which we shall better display the illustrious pedigree of the Lady Margaret Countess of Salisbury, and account for some other incidents which afterwards befel her.

Edward

---

have honoured him with a lineal descent from king Arthur. This popular compliment Henry gave into, and caused his eldest son to be named after that prince. "The king, in honour of the British race, of which himself was, named him Arthur, according to the name of that ancient worthy king of the Britons, in whose acts there is truth enough to make him famous, beside what is fabulous." Lord Bacon's Life of Henry VII.

[b] Our author's great desire to aggrandize his hero, seems to have carried him beyond the truth; since Sir Richard Pole is said by the most accurate writers to have been only a private gentleman of Welsh extraction, though a favourite of the king's, to whom Henry gave the lady Margaret Plantagenet in marriage, according to the wary politicks of that prince, in order to debase the pride of that high-spirited family, which seemed to obscure his own, by matching one of the last of the blood with a person so much beneath her.—Gratiani, one of Pole's flattering biographers, thus speaks of his father, and of Henry's reason for choosing this alliance—" Margaretam

CARDINAL REGINALD POLE.

EDWARD [a] the Third ascended the throne of England in 1327, and having afterwards a numerous issue, that he might raise them to dignities becoming their birth, appointed his eldest son EDWARD to succeed him in the throne, his second son JOHN he made duke of LANCASTER, LIONEL the third was created duke of CLARENCE, and EDMUND the fourth duke of YORK. The two princes of the houses of YORK and LANCASTER had male issue, and it fell out in the year 1400, that HENRY,

---

[a] "TAM non ulli ex regni proceribus ne cujus opes animique regii sanguinis conjugio, extollerentur, sed RICARDO POLO mediocri viro affini suo nuptui dedit, quem inde cubiculo suo præfecit.—Neque hunc alia res quàm quod *quietâ submissâque naturâ esset* provexit; neque in POLI familiâ ante eum magnopere quisquam enituit." Gratiani de casibus Illust. Viror. p. 210. Parif. Edit. 4to.

[c] The good archbishop has taken much pains to shew his ignorance of the English history in this very inaccurate and imperfect account of the two families and factions of YORK and LANCASTER, and their favourite distinctions of the *Red* and *White Roses*; which he dwells upon with much seeming pleasure himself, though the reader will probably be as much tired with this part as the translator was; I might have followed DUDITHIUS's example in his Latin version, and cut short this imperfect tale, but I should not then have translated BECCATELLI but DUDITHIUS. His mistakes are indeed very gross, but every common reader may set them right, who knows, that EDWARD the *Black Prince* died before his father; that LIONEL duke of CLARENCE was elder brother to JOHN of GHENT; and that the Device of the *Two Roses* was not invented till HENRY the VI.'s time.

B 3 afterwards

afterwards called HENRY IV. who was cousin german to RICHARD II. and by him sent into banishment, was by the aid of his partisans, among the nobility called back into ENGLAND, and having defeated Richard, and thrown him into prison, took possession of the sovereignty. From this contest between the two cousins, the nobles who favoured the two parties distinguished their different factions by different devices: those who adhered to the interest of HENRY who was the son of the duke of LANCASTER bore the *Red Rose*, and the partisans of Richard of the house of YORK, *the White*, which became afterwards the distinguishing badges of the houses of YORK and LANCASTER. The crown of England continued in the family of the *Red Rose* till the end of Henry VI.'s reign; who in the year 1461 was dispossessed of the sovereignty by EDWARD IV. of the faction of the *White Rose*. From George duke of CLARENCE, the brother of EDWARD, was descended MARGARET, who was afterwards mother of Cardinal POLE; EDWARD had likewise a daughter named ELIZABETH, who became the wife of HENRY VII. of the faction of the *Red Rose*, who, after an exile of some years spent in FRANCE, was by the assistance of a powerful party recalled into ENGLAND, and having routed and slain RICHARD III. of that name, of the *White Rose*, who was then king, ascended the throne in the year 1486: in him the *Two Roses* were blended together, and that factious distinction was totally sunk, he himself being descended

scended from the house of the *Red Rose*, and his queen from that of the *White*.

FROM this intermarriage between HENRY and ELIZABETH was born Henry VIII. who came to the crown on the death of his father, 1509, and wore it till 1547, fullied as it was in the latter part of his reign with many difgraceful blemifhes, through his unbridled indulgence of every intemperate paffion.

THIS king, in the life-time of his father HENRY VII. was [d] affianced in the year 1502 to CA-
THERINE

---

[d] The expreffion in the Italian, is, *prefa per moglie, married*, but the marriage did not in fact take place till after the time he mentions. The many important confequences that followed from this inaufpicious, not to fay, inceftuous marriage of Henry with his brother's widow, require that the truth, and the date of every fact fhould be fairly ftated: want of correctnefs in our author, which is of no very material confequence, and perhaps only cafual, with regard to fome other parts of Englifh hiftory, may poffibly in the prefent inftance be defigned to miflead his reader, and be not quite fo innocent. The truth of this hiftory in the point before us, is this—Prince Arthur died in *April* 1502 (not 1500) aged full 16. HENRY, if LORD BACON fays true, was not declared *Prince of Wales* till *February* 1503, left his brother's widow might be with child, and bring forth a fon: this not happening, on *December* 26, 1503, a bull of difpenfation was procured by the intereft of HENRY and FERDINAND, of pope Julius II. the profligate fucceffor of the no lefs profligate Alexander VI. to authorize thefe inaufpicious nuptials, fpite of every impediment moral or divine; if, in confequence of this bull, the parties were betrothed; yet within two years HENRY with his father's approbation protefted
againft

THERINE daughter of FERDINAND and ISABELLA, king and queen of SPAIN, which princess had been before married to ARTHUR, Henry's elder brother, who died of a fever at the age of 14, in the year 1500.

OF this marriage, solemnized under the papal dispensation, was born in the year 1511 a son named HENRY, who lived but three months: again in the year 1516 they had a daughter called MARY, who survived them, and through many difficulties made her way at last to the throne of England, and was married to PHILIP, son of the emperor Charles V.

WHEN HENRY and his queen, who then lived in perfect harmony together, perceived they had no farther hopes of a successor but in this their only daughter, they devoted their whole attention to the having her religiously and royally educated; and casting their eyes with this intent among the most illustrious ladies of their court, none pleased them so much, nor seemed so eminently qualified for so great a charge, as the lady MARGARET, mother of REGINALD POLE, a widow lady of distinguished

---

against the legality of his own espousals, *June* 27, 1505, in the presence of the BISHOP of WINCHESTER, though this detested marriage was indeed (by the too prevalent influence of the papal power in the king's council, and his own early prejudice in favour of that dispensing power) publickly solemnized and consummated four years afterwards, *June* 7, 1509, to the bitter repentance of the king, and the utter reproach both of the church and court of ROME.

prudence

CARDINAL REGINALD POLE. 9

prudence and discretion, and of most exemplary piety, besides her royal birth, and near relationship to the king, being cousin-german to his mother, who was daughter to Edward IV. as she was to G. D. of CLARENCE, that king's brother, as was related before. The attachment became still stronger in favour of this lady on account of the very particular affection and regard queen Catherine bore her, whose family, she thought, had a fair claim upon her for their future hopes of the crown, as the innocent blood of the last male heir of it had been barbarously shed to propitiate the rites of her first marriage: for when Henry and Ferdinand were in treaty for a match between their children, some jealousies arose on account of EDWARD earl of WARWICK, nephew to EDWARD IV. the heir of the duke of CLARENCE, and brother to the lady MARGARET, whose pretensions to the crown of England, for reasons not necessary to be enlarged upon, seemed too well founded, and for which only crime he had been kept a prisoner from his childhood, first by the command of his uncle RICHARD III. and afterwards on the same pretence by HENRY VII. it was therefore now resolved that he should be taken off before the * solemnization of

---

* This nefarious contract between the two kings, signed with the blood of an innocent prince, is an indelible stain on the memory of HENRY VII. and was the deadly arrow which stuck in the bosom of Q. CATHERINE to her last hour, and caused that bitter reflection which she made in her sufferings, " She

10 THE LIFE OF

of the marriage with CATHERINE, which resolution was executed by Henry VII. who put him to death in the Tower of LONDON 1499.

QUEEN Catherine was not unacquainted with this event, and had a gentle nature incapable of not feeling remorse on the recollection of it, insomuch that she had been heard to say, "She should not die in peace unless she could be the instrument of restoring to the Plantagenet family some future hopes of succeeding to the crown," intimating by these words her desire of giving her daughter in marriage to one of lady MARGARET's sons, who had [f] all of them a great share in her affection.

"She had not herself offended; but it was the judgment of God, because her former marriage was made in blood." LORD BACON.

[f] The catholic writers, who *imagined* only they had found a suitable match for their zealous QUEEN in the no less bigotted CARDINAL, to make his pretensions (groundless as they ever were) seem more plausible, have gone back even to the childhood of the queen, and her mother's preference in favour of REGINALD, for the first foundation of this tale. THOMAS PHILIPS, POLE's late biographer, has taken up this story of BECCATELLI's (though without acknowleging his authority); but to add to its plausibility in favour of the future cardinal, he has asserted more than BECCATELLI authorized him, when he says—"Amongst all that lady's numerous offspring, the queen had ever shewn a predilection to Reginald." PHILIPS's LIFE OF C. POLE, vol. i. p. 34.

For

CARDINAL REGINALD POLE.

For all these concurrent reasons, the king and queen earnestly solicited this virtuous and pious lady, to undertake the tuition of their only daughter, who in the course of her life discovered many excellent qualities, which she had derived from the sage and pious instructions of her noble governess [s]. Thus much I thought necessary to premise in proof of the Cardinal's illustrious extraction, on his mother's side.

---

[s] A passionate warmth in religious disputes, which made her take a more violent part in the public feuds of Henry VIII. reign than became her sex and station, and a natural vehemence of temper, not always under the curb of discretion, which cast a very blameable indecorum on her last, though bitter sufferings, seem to be the characteristic qualities of the countess of SALISBURY; and they were afterwards as predominant in her pupil MARY——Let us take a short sketch of her character from two catholic writers, very partial in other respects to her memory.

Le caractere d'esprit de MARIE lui inspiroit naturellement cet excés de severité——Je voudrois qu'elle eut plus epargnée le sang, & qu'elle eut fait reflexion que les voyes trop violentes d'induire les peuples au changement, convient à l'erreur non à la veritable foi,

Pere d'Orleans, Revol. d'Angleterre, vol. ii. p. 370.

Cette princesse naturellement fiere & opiniatre s'affirmissoit dans ces desseins par la resistance de ses sujets : elle haissoit les Anglois.

M. l'Abbé de Vertot, Introd. aux Ambassades de Noailles, vol. i. p. 265.

BUT,

But, to resume the thread of my story, let it be remembered that Henry VII. as I said above, having imprisoned and afterwards put to death Edward Plantagenet, brother of Margaret, resolving to place all the present and future hopes of his kingdom in the hands of persons well attached to his interest, thought it expedient to give Margaret, afterwards countess of *Salisbury* [h], in marriage to one of his chief favourites, a gentleman of family in *Wales*, his own native country, and nearly allied to him in blood; his choice fell on Sir Richard Pole, one of the principal knights in his court, who was not only of the Lancastrian party, but his own cousin [i]; to him he gave the

---

[h] Lady Margaret Pole was not created countess of Salisbury till 1513, the 5th of Henry VIII. " on her petition to the " king that she might inherit the state and dignity of her bro- " ther Earl of Warwick, who was attainted the 19th of " Henry VII. and be styled countess of *Sarum*." Ld. Herbert's Life of Hen. VIII.

[i] Sir Richard Pole was avowedly a gentleman of an ancient family in Wales, and very probably a relation to the king on his father's side, tho' from many different accounts of the first rise of the Tudor family, that relationship is not easily to be ascertained: the king, who feared no ambitious attempts from his mild and gentle temper, chose him out as the most eligible match for the Lady M. Plantagenet, and afterwards honoured him with the garter, and intrusted him with the care of his son Prince Arthur. Some historians, either thro' ignorance or flattery, have made him of the family of the De la Pole's, earls and dukes of Suffolk; but later writers have regulated that

the lady MARGARET PLANTAGENET in marriage, who bore him six children, four sons and two daughters; the eldest, who succeeded to his father's inheritance, was called HENRY; the second ARTHUR; REGINALD [k], the subject of our history, was the third, and GEOFFRY the fourth. They all survived their father, and fell young under the care of their mother, by whose discrete management the daughters were finely accomplished, and married into the principal families of the kingdom.

REGINALD was born in March 1500 [l], and by the attention of his mother was trained up to early habits

---

that mistake. See note to Rapin's hist. vol. i. p. 814. T. PHILIPS makes the same mistake in calling the E. of SUFFOLK, who was executed in Hen. VIII's time, POLE, whereas his name was DE LA POLE (vol. i. p. 31).

[k] Beccatelli has not been exact in his account of Sir R. Pole's family: *Dugdale* makes REGINALD the youngest, and places GEOFFRY before ARTHUR.—*T. Philips* says, they had only one daughter named URSULA, so that there now remains but *five* of what he has called (vol. i. p. 34.) "that lady's "*numerous* offspring."

[l] The more illustrious star of Charles V. ascended the hemisphere not many days before (on Feb. 24, 1500) to which POLE was but an humble *Satellite*, still courting Charles's superior influence, yet dreading to approach it.—POLE was born, says CAMDEN, at *Stourton-Castle* in *Staffordshire*, belonging to the family of the earls of *Warwick*, which came into the possession

habits of virtue, and a knowledge of letters suitable to his years; as soon as he was qualified for it she sent him to a Grammar school, kept within the precincts of a *Carthusian* monastery about seven miles from *London*, a very pleasant religious retirement; from whence, after he had laid the foundation of his grammatical knowlege, he was removed to the *University* of *Oxford*, where he applied himself closely to his first course of lectures in logic and ethics, in which he made so uncommon a proficiency as to be able, young as he was, to hold a public disputation in those sciences for 30 days successively [m], except the festivals, on which no public exercises were performed: his principal intimates and preceptors in those studies were Dr. THOMAS LINACER and WILLIAM LATIMER, the two ablest scholars at that time in *England*.

---

session of his mother by the liberality of Henry VIII. (in right of her grandfather RICHARD NEVIL, earl of *Salisbury*) for all whose castles, manors, and lands she obtained a grant, dated Oct. 14, 1514. Dugdale Baron. Vol. ii. p. 292.

[m] DUDITHIUS seems startled at this marvellous feat of logic of young REGINALD's, and therefore softens it a little in his translation, " solennem disputationem *per aliquot dies* habuerit." —It is wonderous A. Wood has not recorded this extraordinary effort of POLE's in his ATHENÆ OXON. who has supplied T. PHILIPS with so many anecdotes less to his honour in several of the 18 pages of his life. Philips's Life of C. Pole, 5 & seq. pages.

HAVING

CARDINAL REGINALD POLE. 15

Having thus made very extraordinary improvements in literature in proportion to his years, at the age of 19 he conceived a strong inclination to visit the *Universities* in ITALY; where, he had heard, the *Belles Lettres*, he had such delight in, were in the highest reputation, and particularly at PADUA. Whereupon, with the king's permission, and the consent of his mother and friends, he embarked for ITALY, and came to PADUA about the year 1520, having procured a stipend from the king, payable out of the exchequer, of 300 *l. per Annum*, equal to 500 *crowns*, besides other revenues of his own to the yearly value of 1000 *crowns* more; the principal part of which arose out of the deanry of OXFORD [n] and other church [o] preferments, which

---

[n] Beccatelli has written by mistake OXFORD instead of EXETER, which was the deanry POLE was promoted to by the resignation of PACE, who was advanced to that of St. Paul's on the death of Dean Collet in 1519; if so, A. Wood must be mistaken when he says, under the article of R. PACE, "He was dean of Exeter, but upon the failure of his understanding resigned it to R. POLE," *Wood's Athenæ Oxon*. Whereas it appears, that PACE, who was then dean of St. Paul's, and king Henry's agent at Venice, was not deprived of his senses till the year 1525. Godwin's Annals.

[o] "This was according to a custom then prevailing (and which the bishops made a fruitless attempt to abrogate the 7th of Edward VI.) that many noblemen and gentlemen's sons had prebends given them, on pretence that they intended to fit themselves by study for holy orders, which they often still retained tho' their studies went no farther." Parl. Hist. Edward VI.

he

he obtained through the courtesy of Dr. Richard Pace, who resigned them in his favour.

Here he provided himself a house, with an establishment suitable to his quality, and commenced an acquaintance with the men of the greatest abilities in that university, who resorted to him daily, pleased with his engaging manners, and the fine talents he disclosed so early. His principal intimate was M. P. Bembo, a noble Venetian, who had left the court of Rome for his health, and was retired to Padua. For his philosophical studies he attended the lectures of N. Leonicus, who was distinguished also for his perfect knowlege of the Greek tongue [p], who brought him well acquainted with the writings of Aristotle and Plato, in their original language. He retained also many learned men in his own family, the chief of whom were Christopher Longolius, a *Fleming*, eminent for the elegance of his style in the Latin tongue, and Thomas Lupset, an *Englishman*, in eloquence, learning, and piety equal to the first of his countrymen. With these aids he made a rapid progress both in the languages and sciences, as ap-

---

[p] A very probable reason for Pole's wishing to go to *Italy* might be, his desire to perfect himself in the *Greek* tongue, in which there was great want of professors in the English universities, as Latimer complains in a letter to Erasmus; wishing some eminent master might be sent from thence, if it were only to instruct Fisher, bishop of *Rochester*, in that language.

pears

pears from some compositions which he wrote about that period, and among others from the *Life of Longolius* [q] who died in his family, which is printed, but without his name, at the beginning of LONGOLIUS's works. In this manner POLE spent his time till the beginning of the year 1525, still adding one improvement upon another, to the great increase of his reputation not in PADUA only, but in VENICE, and thro' all ITALY and the parts adjacent; being mentioned with signal marks of honour in the literary correspondence of the most eminent [r] men of that age, BEMBO, NAVAGERO, ERASMUS, LONGOLIUS, and many others.

On

---

[q] The *Life of Longolius*, which R. POLE wrote at the age of three or four-and-twenty, as a memorial of his regard for a deceased friend, will probably disappoint the expectation of a curious reader, after the passionate encomiums lavished on it by *Pole's late biographer*. If I might venture to criticise it, I would say, It seems neither to breathe the warmth of youthful affection, nor to be animated with any lively strokes of genius or expression; we neither view the spirited young orator describing the quick and astonishing progress in science of his friend and forerunner: nor do we see the tender youth weeping over the bier of a beloved companion untimely taken from him; but we are coldly presented with a grave and uninteresting detail of his birth, family, education, and pursuits, in a style rather embarrassed than elegant, rather pedantic than polite.

[r] CARDINAL QUIRINI (who acknowleges to have taken the *Scheme* of his whole *Diatriba on Pole's Letters* from this short life written of him by BECCATELLI) has fulfilled the duty

On the commencement of the year 1525, having acquired much knowlege and reputation in ITALY, by the follicitation of his mother and the reft of his friends he propofed returning to ENGLAND; but as it was the *Quarter-Jubilee* this year at Rome, he refolved to vifit that city before he fet his face towards his own country. He began his journey with a fmall retinue of his own domeftics, yet he could not travel fo privately, but at FLORENCE, and at many other towns thro' which he paffed, he was received * with every mark of public refpect,

without

---

duty of an elaborate editor, in examining the letters of all thefe men of note in our author's lift, and giving us the whole letter, or fome paffage of it, wherein POLE's name is mentioned with honour: thofe letters, the reader may imagine, have furnifhed the *Cardinal* with the means of enlarging upon many circumftances in the hiftory of POLE or his cotemporaries at PADUA, which Beccatelli thought foreign to his purpofe. He hath taken the pains alfo to collect MINUTES of the lives and characters of POLE's feveral intimates, who were either ftudents or profeffors in the *Italian univerfity* during his abode there, whofe names BECCATELLI has barely mentioned.

If I fhould refer the reader to an original writer for an exact account of Pole's five years fpent at PADUA, he may find it in the *firft chapter of C. Quirini's Diatriba on the firft volume of Pole's Letters*. But if this account from a copyift at fecond hand will fatisfy him, he may read it in the *firft fection of Philips's Life of Pole*, who is, though not in all places, a *tolerable* tranflator of the Cardinal's Latin.

* Not to detract from young Reginald's intrinfic excellencies
with

without knowing to whom he owed the obligation. This distinction (as he afterwards told me) was owing to the singular politeness and courtesy of Gio. Mat. Giberti, bishop of Verona, who, before he was personally known to him, caused those public honours to be paid him, both on his road and upon his arrival at Rome, where he made a very short stay; and having visited only the places sacred to devotion, without appearing at

---

with which he figured so much in the *foreign* university, it may be presumed the national vanity of the Italians helped to blazon them not a little. They were extremely proud of seeing a young student of the blood royal of England grace their schools. He was their idol, not only for his excellence as a scholar, but for the figure he made there through the magnificence of his appointments; his comrades and correspondents were full of puffs on that occasion in all their letters—Bembo calls him *Il Monsignor d'Inghilterra; il più propinquo che habbia quel Rè* (from whence Philips idly imagines that was his usual title). He styles himself, in the life of Longolius, Nobilis Britannus—Erasmus flatters him in the same style, when he recommends him to the acquaintance of the Polish nobleman John a Lasco—*Amabis tui simillimum, clarissimæ majorum imagines, dignitates amplissimæ, spes ampliores.*

† Quirini gives great merit to the modesty of R. Pole, that he did not presume to make himself known at the court of Clement VII. on his passing through Rome at the time of the jubilee 1525. A better reason may possibly be given for his declining it at that time. He had applied to Giberti to recommend him to the pope; he had been very earnest

C 2 with

at the court of CLEMENT VII. he haftened with all expedition to his native country, to the embraces of his friends, and particularly of his mother, who loved him with the greateft tendernefs. He was received with peculiar courtefy by the king and queen, and the whole nation in general; who did honour to the many polite accomplifhments he had acquired in ITALY; yet he did not relax in the leaft from that clofe application to his ftudies to which he had fo long habituated himfelf; but reflecting on the many happy hours he had fpent in his earlier years in that delightful retirement within the walls of the *Carthufian* convent, where DR. J. COLET, a divine of great learning and piety, had built himfelf a very handfome houfe, he procured a grant of it from the king, and made it his place of abode for the two following years.

As foon as HENRY's wicked refolution became public, of abandoning his firft and lawful wife, and marrying another, to which he was ftimulated

---

with BEMBO to know whether his name had yet been mentioned to his HOLINESS; it appears by a letter from BEMBO to him (which was certainly written after the month of February 1525, though it is not dated) that he was not yet certain whether GIBERTI had yet fpoken of him or no; it was not therefore confiftent with POLE's character, however folicitous of fo doing, to have appeared at the court of ROME till this point had been firft cleared up. *P. Bembus R. Polo, Epiftola, Lib.* i. *C. Quirini.*

by his own licentious paffions, and the encouragement of bafe minifters; POLE, foreboding the future calamities of his country, determined to withdraw himfelf; and having obtained the king's [u] permiffion, upon plea of his earneft defire to vifit the *univerfity* of PARIS, with the intire approbation of his mother, he left the kingdom.

DURING his ftay at PARIS the breach between the king and queen grew ftill wider, infomuch that HENRY, to give the greater force to his own paffion for the divorce, by the concurrent approbation of learned cafuifts, fent his emiffaries to collect the opinions of the feveral univerfities in EUROPE, and among the reft he wrote to POLE at PARIS, and

---

[u] BECCATELLI enters upon the ftory of the *Divorce* with the virulence of an inquifitor, and PHILIPS has imbibed no fmall portion of his fpirit, but it is a fubject foreign to my plan, and has been difcuffed by abler cafuifts; yet to clear up the king's generofity in this place with refpect to Pole, I muft obferve, that Beccatelli fays, on Pole's afking leave to quit the kingdom and go to Paris,—*fen' andò con buona grazia fua*—*He went with the free confent of the king*; whereas PHILIPS afferts, without any authority, that "Henry at firft fhewed an unwilling-"nefs, although he afterwards granted his requeft, and con-"tinued the former marks of his favour;" which behaviour of the king's refers to POLE's going afterwards to AVIGNON, and not to his prefent voyage, which he has confounded—And then furely the king had fome reafon to hefitate a little, whether he fhould continue his royal favour to a perfon who had juft before fo grofsly infulted him to his face; though he afterwards as nobly granted, as Pole meanly accepted, his former benevolence.

gave him full powers, in quality of his ambaffador, to procure if poffible the judgment of that univerfity in his favour. REGINALD was thunderftruck at this commiffion, thus to find himfelf driven back into the midft of the ftorm, when he flattered himfelf he was fafe in the harbour. Whereupon he excufed himfelf to the king with his wonted modefty, and pleaded his incapacity of ferving him in an affair which required a perfon more converfant in thofe fciences, which he had never yet made the objects of his ftudies. The king therefore determined to join another of his council with him in that commiffion, whom [w] POLE received with all due courtefy and accommodation at his arrival, and fubmitted the whole conduct of the bufinefs to his [x] management.

POLE

---

[w] This perfon was G. DE BELLAI, as Pole tells us himfelf in his letter to EDWARD VI. *Quirini, vol.* iv. *p.* 313.—It is fomewhat obfervable, that BELLAI does not mention POLE's name as of part with him in this commiffion, when he relates the whole tranfaction as it paffed under his management, both at PARIS and other FRENCH and Italian univerfities. Troifieme Livre des Memoires du M. Bellai, p. 92. fol. edit.

[x] POLE has related this ftory in two different tracts of his publifhed by C. QUIRINI, as far as concerns this particular tranfaction; by which it appears, that he acted an irrefolute, but not an irreprehenfible part in it;—fince he fubmitted to take upon him the character of the king's commiffioner for that Bufinefs, before BELLAI arrived.— *Perfonam ad tempus mihi imponi paffus fum dum alter adeffet*—whatever he did in the conduct

Pole continued at Paris a whole year, at the close of which he was prevailed upon by his relations and friends to leave France, and retire to his former solitude in the monastery of *Shene*[b], where he might pass his time unmolested, and avoid giving any cause of suspicion to the king. This prudent counsel he readily obeyed, and spent two years there with great tranquillity, to the infinite satisfaction of all his friends.

But the impatience of Henry to accomplish the purpose of the divorce being more inflamed

---

duct of it afterwards—nay more, he acknowleges in his letter to Edward VI, that though he endeavoured to keep as clear of it as possible, and gave offence to the king by it, yet he was always looked upon as one of the agents; and when he returned to England, it was to give an account of his conduct in that commission—*Delata mihi res est addito collega* G. Langeio Gallo — *confecto negotio Lutetiâ domum revertissem, ut regi rationem legationis meæ redderem.* Epist. ad Edvard. VI. Quirini, vol. iv. p. 313.

[b] The monastic solitudes of Shene, Rovelone, and Magusa, seem to have suited better with the genius and complexion of Pole than the more busy and active scenes of a court or a council. Here he might have retired with the pious spirit of Colet, and written with the elegant pen of Erasmus. He had filled his character more suitably to the natural bent of his disposition, to have lived and died *The Good Prior of Shene*, than to have presided, The servile tool of the papal power in the council of Trent, or the bloody instrument of Mary's vengeance in the hierarchy of England.

by the opposition he met with from many of his subjects; it was suggested to him, that could he but prevail with REGINALD POLE to recommend it by his concurrence, such was his influence, young as he was, over the rest of the nobility, he could not fail to draw them all over to his opinion. The king approved of this proposal, and began to tamper with POLE's family to use their interest with him on this occasion, promising them at the same time that he would give him the choice of the two best ecclesiastical preferments that were then vacant, *York* or *Winchester*, for which purpose he kept the bishoprick of *Winchester* open for four months; he did the like also by the archbishoprick of *York*, each of which were at that time worth no less than 30,000 [c] *crowns per annum*. REGINALD's brothers, and others of his friends, were engaged to carry this point with him, though he shewed the greatest

---

[c] The archbishop of *Ragusa* seems not to have well understood the value of the bishopricks and archbishopricks in ENGLAND, though he may have erred perhaps in his several valuations not without design. He enhances the price of the magnificent temptations which POLE resisted, to do greater honour to his self-denial; so that the archbishoprick of YORK is now called worth 30,000 crowns——He depreciated the value of the archbishoprick of *Canterbury* afterwards, when it was given to POLE; and reckoned it but at the yearly income of 12,000 crowns, almost a third less than *York*, to account for the necessity of the queen's further bounty, and to make the 3000 DUCATS, which were defalcated for his use from the fee of *Winchester*, appear less reproachable.

reluctance

reluctance on his part; but upon their earnest solicitations with him, to gratify the king in some degree, who had given him so many marks of his affection, and not to provoke him so far by his obstinate silence as to bring ruin upon himself and his family; he gave them this answer, after many fruitless excuses: " I cannot gratify my friends at " the expence of my own conscience, but I will " do some violence to myself rather than not sa- " tisfy all parties." This answer of POLE appeared so flattering to their hopes, that they immediately reported to the king, that Pole would comply. HENRY was so well pleased with this information, that he treated him afterwards with uncommon courtesy and affability; but POLE, as was usual with him, having recourse to God in prayer for a full resolution of his doubts, could never reconcile himself to a compliance with the king's desires, as they seemed to him both sinful in themselves, and contradictory to the laws of the church. He determined therefore to speak his sentiments without reserve, and address the king not as a flatterer, but as a faithful counsellor and relation, so that he might obey the truth when he saw it fairly laid open to him. This task he afterwards performed with much eloquence and modesty, but took care that none but the king should be privy to his sentiments on this occasion. When therefore nothing remained to be done more, *he went to*

---

a C. QUIRINI, and his *Translator* T. Philips, exult greatly upon *to the king,* who expected him with impatience, having reason to hope he came to speak in favour of

---

upon REGINALD's behaviour at this remarkable interview between HENRY and him, and reproach Bishop BURNET for not giving credit to an incident so well attested by both POLE's biographers, BECCATELLI and DUDITHIUS, and related by himself in two *tracts* of his own, his *Epist. ad Edv.* VI. and *Apologia ad Parliam.* Three out of the four of these he may be supposed to have known nothing of, as they were MSS. little heard of till C. QUIRINI and SCHELHORN published them. It seems indeed somewhat extraordinary that DUDITHIUS's life of POLE should have escaped so extensive a reader as BURNET, since the *Venetian Edition of* 1563 was almost in every public library before *Wharton's Editions* either of 1690 or 1696 were known to the world: however that be, the bishop's disbelief of the story redounds to the honour of the king, as he supposes HENRY could not have behaved so liberally and indulgently to POLE as he did afterwards, had POLE dared to have insulted him personally in the manner this story relates.

The truth of the interview can now indeed no longer be doubted; the circumstances of which T. PHILIPS has patched together from the *Diatriba* of C. *Quirini, vol.* i. *ch.* 3. who has given us the four several relations of it that occur in BECCATELLI, DUDITHIUS, the LETTER to ED. VI. and the APOL. AD PARL. from a comparison of all which it seems most evident, that the king's behaviour was manly, sensible, and generous; POLE's, irresolute, frantic, and ridiculous; the see of York had been kept open a month, either by the request of himself or his friends, till he could get over some scruples as to the terms upon which it was offered him. The time elapsed— He promised the king satisfaction—His audience was appointed—His friends waited the promised hour of his compliance and consequent promotion, with impatience—It came—The king

of his cause. The king was alone, and admitted him with a most gracious countenance into his privy-chamber; upon which, with the most humble reverence, and testimony of duty to his majesty, he represented to him the true state of the question, and intreated him to inquire more fully into the merits of the case, and not ruin his immortal soul, and blot that fair reputation which had hitherto graced his character. The Cardinal has since told me, he observed the king's features became disordered on a sudden, that his countenance instantly changed, and he put his hand to his dagger which he wore by his side; but, recollecting himself immediately, he said only, " *I will* ° *consider what you have said,*
" and

---

king received him most graciously——But——he broke out into the severest reflections on that very motion he came to give his assent to: " *Cœpissem* (said he) *omnia dicere quæ tam sententiam oppugnarent, cujus defensor expectatus veneram.*"——Henry, upon this behaviour, which seemed more like that of a madman than a candidate for a bishoprick, recoiled with surprise, but soon recollecting himself, dismissed him his presence with a proper contempt; yet, notwithstanding the heinousness of the affront, he condescended soon to pardon him, and suffered him to enjoy the pension he had hitherto granted him, with a generosity that must be ever mentioned to the honour of the king, and the disgrace of REGINALD.

° This story (although thus related by BECCATELLI with every incident in favour of POLE) can never do him credit with a sensible examiner; he prevaricated with his prince; he deceived his friends; he acted disingenuously in himself; but he was forgiven——He wept, and remained still a pensioner——I must
remark

" and you shall have my answer;" and dismissing him angrily from his presence, he never sent for him more. The king said afterwards to some of his lords, he was so incensed against him at the time, he had it frequently in his heart to have struck his poniard into him during the interview; but there was so much simplicity in his manner, that it checked his indignation, and he could not think he really meant him any ill, though he had thus offended him beyond measure.

After this harsh encounter with the king, when he found himself fallen under the discountenance both

---

remark only before I leave it, a variation in two MSS. of this passage in Beccatelli, which sets Reginald's behaviour in a still worse light. The words *andò al Re, he went to the king*, are, in the most antient MS. of the two, *portò la sua scrittura al Re, he carried a written paper to the king*; and again, *Io considererò questa vostra opinione*, in the king's answer to him, *I will consider what you have said*, is written, *Lasciatemi la scrittura, ch' io la vedro*, " Leave your paper with me, and I will consider it."

C. Quirini allows this latter the more ancient reading, though he imagines indeed with his friend who communicated it to him (from a collection of MSS. in a family of the Beccatelli's, collateral descendants of our author at Bologna) that Beccatelli himself afterwards altered it in the manner it now stands in the later Vatican MS.—But if the more ancient text be the right one, it is then clear, Pole had written down his opinion before he went to his audience with the king, and carried it with him: if so, what becomes of that instantaneous impulse of the Holy Spirit, which, he tells Edw. VI. in his letter, forced him to utter words diametrically opposite to his

own

both of Henry and many of the [f] court, POLE resolved to get leave if possible to quit the kingdom, and retire to one of the foreign universities, before any worse consequences befel him. This permission he obtained by a judicious application to some persons in favour; nay, so placable was the king himself towards him, that he would not withdraw any part of the appointment which he had before allowed him, and which had been regularly paid to him ever since its first allotment. He then took leave of his mother, and passed over into FRANCE; and that he might be as distant as possible, he went into the remotest part of it, to the university of AVIGNON in PROVENCE, in the jurisdiction of the

---

own preconceived thoughts and intentions before he went into the king's presence?

[f] Beccatelli is more ingenuous in assigning the true and plain reason for Pole's leaving England with so much precipitation the third time, and retiring into the remote parts of France; viz. "the king's and kingdom's general displeasure upon his "late duplicity of behaviour, and the personal affront shewn "to the king," than Pole himself was, when he tells the emperor in his RHETORICAL APOLOGY (where there is more flourish than solid truth) "he left his country upon observing "CROMWEL's growing interest with Henry,"—subitum discessum meum, ut eum in authoritate apud regem crescere videbam; statim enim patriam reliqui eo tempore, quo maxime frui debebam, & desiderabam— Apologia ad Carol. vol. i. p 132. QUIRINI. This assertion of POLE's, however false, T. PHILIPS adopts at random, and translates it, "This pro- "spect cautioned him to leave *a second time* (he should have "said *a third time*) a hostile land,' vol. i. p. 72.

holy

holy see. Here he staid almost a year; but finding the bleak exposure of that place too sharp for him, he resolved for PADUA [e], where he had before enjoyed a perfect state of health, and been greatly respected. This resolution he put in practice in 1532, at which time I had the fortune to be resident in that university—He divided his time between PADUA and VENICE, distinguished in both places for his modest and amiable carriage, and devoted his whole attention to THEOLOGICAL studies. During his abode there, he kept up a constant correspondence with men of the first note, who both loved and respected him; the chief of these were, the Lord PIETRO BEMBO, M. TRIPHON GABRIELI, MARC ANTONIO GENUA, LAMPRIDIO OF CREMONA, LAZARO OF BASSANO, and other *literati*; but his principal intimates were those who were engaged in the same course of religious

---

[e] Pole, in his treatise *de Unitate Ecclesiæ*, lib. iii. c. 3. casts many illiberal reflections upon both the English and foreign universities, for prostituting their judgment in favour of the *divorce*.—His favourite Padua made her decision in approbation of it, July 1, 1530, which was formally attested by the PODESTA, who affirms, " Eleven doctors were present, and the " determination was made by the unanimous consent of the " whole body"—It was marvellous he could submit within two years afterwards to honour that university with his presence, if she had thus debased herself in his sight by so shameful a prostitution. Either therefore PADUA was not so culpable, or POLE was too prodigal of his censures; for, however calm his deportment might be, his pen was at all times very sharp and unguarded.

exercises,

exercises, which caused him to bear a singular attachment to Cosmo Gherio, bishop of Fano, who followed his divinity-studies there at that time, and, young as he was, was esteemed by all as the very *Mirror* [a] *of learning and politeness.* Not inferior was his regard for M. Alvise [b] Priuli, a Venetian gentleman of fine parts and learning, who engaged in so strict a friendship with R. Pole from his first knowlege of his many amiable qualities,

---

[a] The grateful temper of Beccatelli prompted him to scatter this little incense upon the ashes of his deceased friend and patron the bishop of Fano as he passed on, in whose retinue he came first to Padua 1528, and was probably part of his houshold till the untimely loss of this his *first* friend in 1537, after which he joined himself to Contarini, and upon his decease, to Cardinal Pole. I should conjecture, from Beccatelli's peculiar talent for biography, which he exerted with great gratitude to the memory of his two successive patrons, Contarini and Pole, that he was also the author of a MS. which C. Quirini says is extant in the Magliabecchian library at Florence, intituled, *Vita e Costumi del Reverendo Monsignor Vescovo di Fano*, though the author be not mentioned; especially as it is there said to have been written at the instance of A. Priuli, who was Beccatelli's most intimate friend.

[b] *Alvise Priuli Gentilhuomo Venetiano*, is the only title by which Beccatelli has distinguished Pole's intimate friend and his own. Had he been, what Dudithius (and Philips after him) calls him, a *noble Venetian*, Beccatelli would certainly not have abridged him of his honours. Why Alvise Priuli should be called Aloysius Priuli, partly by the Latin appellation, and partly by the Italian, I can't devise—He who knew his own name, called himself always Alvise Priuli in his Italian letters, and Aloysius Priolus in his Latin.

that

that he would never leave him afterwards, but followed him in all his fortunes, as will be related in the progress of this history. At VENICE he became very intimately connected with the illustrious G. CONTARINI, who was afterwards a cardinal, and with the archbishop of TEATI [k], who had there a seminary of *religious* under his tuition, which he was establishing on a stricter plan of discipline. Such were POLE's studies, and such his associates at PADUA and VENICE; and in this interval it happened, as he was weeping over the miseries of his country, which were filling up their measure every day, to consummate its wretchedness, the king took it into his head to break off from his allegiance to the church, as he had before done from his queen, and to set himself up as head and *pope* [1] in ENG-

---

[k] This sect of the rigid CARAFFA's institution, which made great external pretensions to extraordinary sanctity, is humourously described by Bishop Hall, Sat. VII. Book IV.

— a false dissembling THEATINE,
Whose brawny skin is red with shirts of mail,
And rugged hair-cloth scours his greasy nail —

[1] Beccatelli seems rather quaint than serious in his anger against HENRY, when he tells us, "The devil put it into his head to separate from the church, as he had from his wife, and turn *pope* of England." What would he have said to CHA. V. who was so much more under the delusion of Satan, that (as Mr. Bayle tells the story) " afin de gouter de toutes sortes de " dominations, aspira à etre PAPE;" not *pope* of ENGLAND, or *pope* of SPAIN, but *pope* of ROME; but that he was ashamed to

ENGLAND. Such influence has the malice of men, or rather of the devil, on minds corrupt as his was. And to prevent his good kinsman from enjoying any tranquillity, though removed to so great a distance, he sent a courier to him express in 1535, to demand his opinion in writing on this his new title of *Supreme Head of the Church of England*, and to assure him, that he would on no account dispense with a refusal. This message, seconded by letters from his friends, and from the principal persons about the court, greatly disconcerted him, as he well knew these were but as so many snares [m] set to intangle him, and draw him into some treasonable expressions against the king, whose resentment was now raging with all its fury against his best [n] subjects,

---

fit in the same chair with those men of holy names, but impious morals, ALEXANDER VI. and JULIUS III.

[m] If HENRY really meant to draw POLE into a snare, and seduce him into some expressions of disaffection to the crown by the task he imposed upon him, sure never silly bird flew more blindly into the net; for every licentious expression of abuse, every possible term of insolence, provocation, and defiance, that could misbecome a sovereign to hear, and a subject to utter, are lavished through every page of that NOTABLE PHILIPPIC, which cost the precipitate pen of POLE but four months in composing, so impatient was he to write himself A TRAITOR!

[n] Neither the stormy spirit of those times, nor the impetuous genius of HENRY, *which rode in that whirlwind*, can be supposed

jects, and had fallen upon many, in particular upon Sir THOMAS MORE and the BISHOP OF ROCHESTER. On the other hand he reflected, that it might be the divine pleasure to make this trial of his stedfastness, and that he might possibly be an instrument of some good to the king and kingdom. He therefore sat himself down to write, and in four months finished the work which is now published *On the Unity* º *of the Church*, which he transmitted to the king by an English gentleman of his houshold, with orders to deliver it into his majesty's own

---

posed to have been regulated by the sober plan of strict moral rectitude; yet it may be said with truth, that the unfortunate bishop of *Rochester* fell rather a victim to the ill-timed distinction of PAUL III. than to the resentment of HENRY VIII. His confirming on him the Cardinalate of *St. Vitale* during his imprisonment, was a challenge to the king to bring him to a trial, were it but for his own vindication, as this act of the POPE's towards one under the censure of the laws, was the most insolent arraignment of the justice of Henry's conduct, and the highest indignity he could offer to the majesty of the English laws. Lord Herbert—Godwin.

º I have given the general title that treatise was called by, though BECCATELLI gives it a name more descriptive of the subject of it, when he calls it, " *Libro della Prestanza della* " *Chiesa, & dei disordini di quel Rè*; A book upon the pre-emi-" nence of the church, and the inordinancy of that king;" a title very characteristic of the abuses it is fraught with against HENRY, and the extravagant arguments it advances in support of the church of *Rome*'s supremacy.

hands,

hands, that no one else might [p] see it, unless it was the king's pleasure.

It

---

[p] Cardinal QUIRINI and *his translator* T. PHILIPS much insist (in excuse for the indecent scurrility with which POLE treats his sovereign, and his benefactor, in this book *De Unitate Eccles.* &c.) that it was drawn up only for his private perusal, and that POLE took such caution in his instructions to the messenger by whom he sent it, as BECCATELLI here mentions, *acciocbe non lo lasciosse vedere non piacendogli.* Nay, R. POLE himself, in his *Apologia ad Parliament. Angliæ*, inserted in Quirini's first vol. p. 179, & seq. in reply to their deserved reproaches for so infamous a libel, avails himself of this excuse. *Ad eum certe solum misi*, &c. But if there be any force in conviction, POLE was assuredly guilty of an equivocation in this point very unworthy of his character.

Pole had sent the whole work at different times thro' Priuli's hand to cardinal Contarini for his examination; just as Priuli was setting out to return from *Rome* to *Venice* with the MS. copy, after it had undergone the perusal of that *cardinal*, Contarini detained him in hopes of procuring POLE's leave to shew it to the pope. Priuli writes for that permission—Let us see POLE's answer. Quirini, vol. i. Epist. 28.

—" *Scribis Reverendissimum cupere, si per me liceat, ut Pontificii ostendat quæ scripsi per me quidem semper licebit, quicquid illi visum fuerit imperare, quin nihil magis cupio quam ut Pontifex legat, nam perlegere scio majoris momenti negotia eum nullo modo permissura*," Permission being once given in so ample a manner to the person who requested it so earnestly, whatever softening excuses he might insinuate afterwards would be only set down to the modesty of the author, and were not likely to prevent Contarini's doing what he was so strongly bent upon.

It happened not long before this time that Paul III. sent for G. Contarini to Rome, having lately promoted him to the cardinalate, to advise with him on some proper plan for restoring the discipline of the church. The resolution agreed

---

both to gratify the pope, and for the future interest of his friend REGINALD.

That Paul III. did consequently see this performance, seems evident from his expressions in the *Brief of Summons* which he sent POLE the JULY following—Te de cujus nobilitate doctrina ac probitate, sinceraque in religionem & Dei ECCLESIAM mente cum EX OPERIBUS TUIS tum fide dignorum testimonio accipimus—Paulus Papa R. Polo Anglo, dat. Roma xix Julii, MDXXXVI.

That PAUL III. alluded to this work *De Unitate* in the above *Summons*, and had also read it, POLE himself confirms in a letter he wrote to GIBERTI bishop of Verona just after he had received the pope's orders.

Ecce, unde minimum expectabam, a PONTIFICE litteræ—Pontifex vult, ut videtur periculum mei facere, utrum quod *verbis* tantopere asseverarim, *de ejus authoritate & vinculo nostræ obedientiæ*, re ipsa præstare velim—vol. i. epist. 43. Quirini.

Does it not now appear by every possible testimony, that the POPE had seen as much of this work of POLE's as he had leisure or inclination to read; nay, that it was upon the merit of that performance that he was so soon after called to Rome to assist at the *Riforma?*—Had not then both HENRY and his PARLIAMENT sufficient cause to exclaim against him, for representing the king his master in such opprobrious colours to the principal enemy of his person and kingdom?

upon

upon was, to call together a sufficient number of persons, eminent for their abilities and integrity, who should, without any respect to worldly considerations, suggest to his holiness the most effectual methods to accomplish this purpose. REGINALD POLE was thought worthy to be named in this list, as CONTARINI had long known his unblemished virtue and probity. Whereupon briefs were dispatched into different parts, to summon those persons agreed upon, who were then absent from ROME: to *Carpentras* for JAC° SADOLET, bishop of that see; to *Venice*, for the archbishop of CHIETI, founder of the order of THEATINES, GREGORIO CORTESE, abbot of *St. George*, and REGINALD POLE: to *Verona*, for GIO. MAT. GIBERTI, bishop of that city; and to *Ugubbio*, for FRED° FREGOSO, archbishop of *Salerno*. The two prelates of *Chieti* and *Verona*, the ABBOT, and POLE, travelled together, and were all received by his *holiness*, on their arrival, with great marks of respect, who was particularly pleased with Reginald's agreeable carriage, and appointed him apartments in his own palace.

THESE honourable *deputies*, in conjunction with some others, drew up a scheme for *a reform*, which was afterwards proposed in full consistory, but by some impediment or other was never put in execution.

This excellent plan [q], subscribed by the several *deputies*, is now extant among the *Volumes of Councils*.

The feast of Christmas now approached, in honour of which the Pope had resolved to make a promotion of CARDINALS, and had marked out REGINALD POLE for one, in regard of his own

---

[q] T. PHILIPS takes up a mistake of QUIRINI's (who says, that BECCATELLI and DUDITHIUS enumerate this *Consilium cardinalium delectorum*, &c. among *Pole's works*, which is not true of either of them—C. Quirini, vol. i. p. 370.) and asserts, at a venture, LIFE OF POLE, vol. i. p. 140. "That Pole "was the directing mind that guided the whole, and alone "drew up the *Plan of the Reformation*." Had he taken time to examine *Beccatelli's Life of Contarini*, where a fuller account is given of the NOVEMVIRATE called together by Paul III. he would have been less forward in his assertion; for there we read, that CONTARINI was *the directing mind*. The plan was his; the persons assembled were of his selecting; upon the grounds of his SANTI RICORDI did they proceed—" In tanto "fervore della Riforma l'aveano posto i santi ricordi del Rev. "Contarino. Quei Signori fedelmente congregandosi quasi "ogni giorno alla stanza del Cardinale, esseguirono la commis- "sione *di sua Beatitudine* come anche hoggi si vede in alcuni "libri"—Beccatelli, through the whole section, gives the chief merit of this work to CONTARINI, which he probably must be thoroughly informed of, being one of that cardinal's family, and most likely then at Rome with him; so that if Pole had been so principal a manager in that *Council of cardinals*, as T. PHILIPS supposes, BECCATELLI would infallibly have mentioned it in one of the two lives, either CONTARINI's or POLE's. Vita del Card. Contarini, sect. xii.

personal

CARDINAL REGINALD POLE.

personal merits, as well as the dignity of his birth, and his connections with ENGLAND: having communicated his resolutions to CONTARINI and other men of note, they were received by every one with the highest approbation, especially by the IMPERIAL MINISTERS, who were very earnest for his success, either because it might promote their master's interest, and enable him by the influence of POLE, seconded by the authority of the see of ROME, to give the affairs of ENGLAND what turn he pleased; or because they should be highly gratified in seeing POLE become a member of the church, as it would put an end to a suspicion entertained by some, that the princess MARY of ENGLAND might possibly some time or other be induced to marry him, from the early acquaintance she had with him, and the affection she had borne him from *her* * childhood.

---

* *Sin da fanciullo* (which is the reading in the *Italian*) would mean POLE's *childhood*; but, if it were so, MARY must have been in love with him in her cradle, as he was 16 years older than she was. C. QUIRINI, when he quotes this passage, alters the original, I know not with what authority, to *sin da fanciullina*; which I have followed, as it makes sense of the passage, tho' not more credibility in the story. DUDITHIUS omits the whole paragraph; but T. PHILIPS adds somewhat more to it, and quotes Beccatelli as saying, what he never says, " that both she and the queen, her mother, had borne him singular affection from *his* infancy," vol. i. p. 141. so that, by PHILIPS's account, she must have loved him some years before she was born.

REGINALD

The LIFE of

REGINALD himself was the only objector to this promotion, which he opposed with great modesty and plainness; representing to his *holiness*, that such a dignity would at this juncture be very unseasonable [b], as it would destroy all his influence in ENGLAND, where every body [c] would be ready to suspect

---

[b] It is impossible for any one, who sits down to read C. POLE's Life and Writings without being possessed of that extravagant Ενθουσιασμος (which one of his friends remarked in his composition, *Quirini*, vol. ii. epist. 8.) with which he lived and wrote, to comprehend the meaning of his arguments on almost any subject, which seem altogether wild and contradictory, and either far beneath, or rather beyond the usual flight of truth and soberness. For instance, Beccatelli here relates, ' He objected with great modesty to Paul III's in-
' tended promotion of him to the cardinalate, as a very un-
' seasonable step, and what would destroy all his influence in
' England.' To the parliament of *England*, who remonstrated with him on his accepting it, he replies, with a warmth of asseveration that shocks one.———' Si aliquid in terris præter
' honorem vestrum, utilitatem vestram me movebat ut ac-
' ciperem, me non recusare ut a cœlis perpetuò excludar.'
Quirini Apol. ad Parl. vol. i. sect. 6.

[c] T. PHILIPS assures his readers, in his preface to his Life of R. POLE, p. x, that ' as several particulars relating to the CARDINAL's public transactions are preserved amongst our own records, access has been had to all of them, and on these authorities whatever is here related rests.' If this be true, he should have referred us to some more authentic record, than either his own or even POLE's bare assertion, for a proof,
' That

suspect he would be too much biassed to the interest of the papal see; besides the manifest ruin it would bring on his own family. He therefore intreated his holiness to leave him, at least for the present, where he was; that so signal a mark of his favour, of which he had the highest sense, might on some future occasion be less hazardous in the acceptance of it, than at that critical period. The Pope seemed satisfied with his apology for waving it, and promised to postpone it for the present, which, I can vouch, was greatly to POLE's satisfaction; but

---

'That both houses of parliament wrote him a letter, to which *each* of the members (according to his own strange phrase) put their name, reproving him for his work of the *Church's Unity*, his accepting of the cardinalate, and making *Rome* his residence.' *Life of Pole*, vol. i. p. 185.

Whereas his sole authority, till he produces a better one, seems to rest on R. POLE's first sentence of his *Apologia ad Parlamentum*, published by C. QUIRINI, vol. i. p. 179, &c.

But what if this *Apology to the English Parliament* be (as Quirini, who published it, has very properly called it) no more than a mere *Rhetoricus Schematismus*, a vehicle to display his talents for oratory, a supposed answer to an imaginary remonstrance? since it is scarce probable the parliament of *England* should stoop from its dignity to engage in a parly with a romantic, hot-brained renegade of five-and-thirty, who had just shewn himself so indecent a scribler in writing a libel upon his prince, which was likely to be noticed in higher terms of resentment by so august a body, than by entering into a correspondence of equality, and subscribing the names of both houses to a letter of remonstrance to a young cardinal.

whether

whether Providence ordained it otherwise, or whether the Imperial party insisted on carrying their point, on the very morning upon which the consistory was to be held for the investiture of the other cardinals, and a resolution was taken to leave REGINALD out of the list, the Pope, after the meeting was convened, changed his mind, and calling to *Durante*, his master of the privy chamber, dispatched him immediately to POLE's apartment, with orders to conform himself implicitly to his holiness's pleasure, and prepare for his investiture by receiving the clerical tonsure.

I happen'd to be with R. POLE when *Durante* brought the message, and the *barber* [d] with him who was to officiate on this occasion. The good man, little expecting such a summons, was the more confused when he heard it, and discovered great tokens of concern in his countenance; but as the time was short, and there was no room for farther remonstrance, *as a sheep before his shearer*, &c. he resigned himself; and on the 22d of *December* MDXXXVI he was proclaimed CARDINAL with XI

---

[d] BECCATELLI (who had attended C. CONTARINI to *Rome*, and was witness to every whimsical circumstance of POLE's behaviour there, while the cardinal's hat hung suspended over his head) seems to dwell on every incident of this tale with an exactness that is very ludicrous, and has given us a scene between the *Candidate for the Cardinalate*, the *Chamberlain*, and the *Barber*, equal to any comic adventure in *Gil Blas*.

CARDINAL REGINALD POLE. 45

more, among whom were the archbishop of SIPONTO, the lords bishops CHIETI, SADOLETI, CARPI, and others.

WITHIN a few days after his promotion, which was to the general satisfaction of the whole consistory, he was appointed *legate*, and received orders to depart immediately for the coasts of *France* and *Flanders* to keep up the spirit[e] of the popish party in *England*, an enterprize to which Paul III. had been encouraged both by the emperor and the king of *France*. The latter, having promised the cardinal a safe-conduct thro' his kingdom, who thereupon undertook the expedition, more out of zeal to bring back HENRY within the pale of the

---

[e] The expression in the Italian is very strong, *per dar fomento a' catholici in Ingliterra*, a very meritorious enterprize for a young cardinal! and a very explicit comment upon the letter he is supposed by T. PHILIPS to have written to the English parliament just before he set out on this expedition, wherein he tells them, ' Vestrâ ergo causâ venio, vestri honoris, & utilitatis causâ,' *Quirini Apolog. ad Parlamentum*, vol. i. p. 186. The *honour* he meant them was, to foment the divisions of their country; the *advantage* he proposed them was, to bring them back under the papal yoke, or spirit up insurrections in every province of the kingdom.

What an English house of commons would, in a more enlightened age, determine upon *such* a letter and *such* an embassy may probably be conjectured; if they pardoned him the *treason*, it would be only in compassion to his being a *madman*.

catholic

catholic church, than from any hostile disposition towards him. Thus invested with full powers, and accompanied with a sumptuous train of attendants, he left *Rome* the beginning of Lent, and prevailed on M. GIBERTI, bishop of *Verona*, who had great address in the conduct of business, and was his particular friend, to bear him company. He was received with great courtesy on his arrival at *Paris* both by the king and clergy; but at the instigation of the king of *England*, who had sent a [f] messenger express to FRANCIS to beg he might be delivered into his hands, he was constrained to leave *Paris* the very next day, the king guarding at the same time against a breach of promise given to the POPE for the CARDINAL's safety, and also avoiding to give offence to HENRY, by ordering POLE to depart [g] immediately out of his kingdom. The cardinal,

---

[f] This application of Henry VIII. to the king of *France* to deliver POLE into his ambassador's hands, was resented by the cardinal as a great indignity. Pope LEO X. thought it no injustice to make the like request to the elector of *Saxony* not 20 years before, to put LUTHER into the hands of his legate CAJETAN. Was the reformer LUTHER amenable to the court of the ROTA for preaching treason against *indulgencies?* and the *traitor-cardinal* privileged against every jurisdiction, tho' he sent a libel to his king, an insolent remonstrance to the legislature, and came down on the frontiers of his country to encourage insurrections against the government?

[g] This unsuccessful mission of the poor cardinal's on his first launching into the political world, shewed the formidable dignity

CARDINAL REGINALD POLE.

dinal, reflecting on the danger of his situation, determined to get out of the *French* territories with all possible speed, before any new resolutions could be formed against him; prudently judging that the sooner he withdrew, the less time would the king of *England* have to devise any stratagem to intercept him.

There was at that time a great number of troops on the frontiers of *Picardy*, who scoured the borders that separate *France* from *Flanders*, and the territories which were at that time in the possession of the *English* army, on account of the war then subsisting between *France* and the emperor. In this hazardous situation the cardinal, submitting

---

dignity of the English king in the principal court of Europe, and the contemptible insignificancy of a popish legate (even when the triple crown had lost less of its splendour than it has since) tho' invested with all the power and parade of his master. The mortification he felt on the cavalier treatment he met with at the court of *France*, breaks out in his letter of complaint to the pope's nuncio at *Paris* soon after he had left that city; in the whole of which there is more anger and less modesty than C. QUIRINI or PHILIPS will allow.

Non possum non maxime obstupescere tantâ regis *christianissimi* patientiâ, qui vel eos qui id petierent audire posset, vel tam turpi postulatione majestatem suam contemni, non ægrius ferret. *Quirini*, vol. ii. ep. 17.

Whoever reads this whole letter will laugh at all T. Philips's endeavours to soften the cardinal's distress and palliate his behaviour, as idle and ridiculous.

himself

himself to the guidance of Providence, took the shortest route to *Cambray*, a neutral territory, subject to the bishop of that see, where he arrived safe, tho' not without great danger; and having staid there a few days, finding his safety would be very precarious, and the bishop too irresolute to be trusted, he resolved to seek some other place of greater security, especially when he heard the king of *England* had proclaimed [h] him a traitor, and set

---

[h] Cardinal POLE complains in his letters to Paul III. and Roderigo Pio, the French nuncio, of the ignominious treatment he had met with from the king of *England*, who proclaimed him traitor, and put a price upon his head. But, if an open avowal of holding correspondence with subjects in actual rebellion, and an attempt to succour and foment their disturbances by coming in person to encourage them, be treason, POLE's own confession will convict him; when, writing to the POPE on the ill success of his embassy, he desires to be recalled, " as the whole scheme he embarked " upon was defeated by HENRY's success against the catholic " insurgents."

Causa ipsa quæ sola me retinere posset, & quæ huc sola traxit, ne spem quidem ullam ostendere videtur, vel minimo periculo dignam cur in his locis diutius maneam, *Populi tumultu qui causam istam fovebat ita sedato*, ut multi supplicio sint affecti (Reg. Polus Paulo III. papæ.) *Quirini*, vol. ii. ep. 19.

And yet, notwithstanding this declaration of the traiterous purpose of his embassy, he wrote at this very time a letter to LORD CROMWEL, the minister he pretended to abhor, " to " clear himself from the imputation of disloyalty, and to pro- " test he had no intention of disservice to the king." Lord Herbert, p. 414.

a price

CARDINAL REGINALD POLE. 47

a price of 50,000 crowns upon his head [1]: Having therefore received an invitation from EVERARD LA MARE, cardinal bishop of *Liege*, with the assurance that his person should be as safe under his protection as his own, he accepted his offer, and was received by him with all the kindness and affection of a brother. Here he staid till the expiration of the six [k] months since his departure from *Rome*, in expectation

---

[1] If every possible incitement to sedition that *words* can give, be not a sufficient proof of treason, yet (to use the cardinal's own expression) se ci fosse chi li confirmasse, o sollecitasse, non solo *con le parole*, ma ancora *con fatti*—If one of the most offensive overt-acts of treason that can be perpetrated, viz. " The supplying rebels with money deliberately raised, " and sent to them to support them in their hostilities against " their sovereign," be proved against Pole, his clamour against Henry will but retort the greater infamy upon himself; of this, his own MEMORIAL given in to the POPE, in the form of INSTRUCTIONS relative to the embassy he was going upon, will sufficiently convict him:

Ma Padre Santo, una cosa non voglii ommettere che mi pare importantissima—quando i popoli non stessero saldi, overo essendo inutili a suscitarli, penso che saria una gran provisione, se ci fosse chi in nome de Vossignoria li confirmasse, o sollecitasse non solo con le parole ma ancora con fatti, i quali bisogneria che fossero, di quella quantita di danari che il bisogno portasse.

Instruzzionne sopra la cose d'Inghilterra data dal C. Polo a Papa Paolo III. Quirini, vol. ii. p. cclxxiv.

[k] BECCATELLI and DUDITHIUS, when they both mention the legate's *six* months stay in FLANDERS, begin their computation from his departure from ROME in Lent, and close it with

expectation that the emperor and the *French* king would fulfil their engagements with him, by doing their utmost to foment the disturbances raised by the malecontents in *England*; whereas their whole attention was taken up in trafficking for themselves, striving which should offer the most tempting purchase for the friendship of the king of *England*, who had the art to establish his own power by keeping up their divisions, and cajoling each of them in their turn, as best suited his purpose. The cardinal of *Liege* assured POLE, that HENRY had offered the states of *Flanders*, of which he was a member, 10,000 foot-soldiers [1] with ten months pay, to carry on the war with *France*, if they

---

with his return thither in the autumn of 1537. T. PHILIPS might therefore have spared his *accurate* correction, when he tells us, in contradiction to his guides, POLE's ancient biographers, " His stay at Liege was about *three* months, viz. " from the beginning of June to the 21st of August 1737." Life of Pole, vol. i. p. 203.

[1] The reader will not wonder if POLE's grateful secretary BECCATELLI sets a higher price on his master, than his other biographers. He tells us, " HENRY offered a reward of " 50,000 crowns for his head:" the depreciator PHILIPS has basely reduced it to 15,000, though both DUDITHIUS and GRATIANI have fixed it at the original price—In the place before us, he assures us, " HENRY would have given 10,000 " men in exchange for him;" whereas PHILIPS sets him so low, as to make him of equal value with no more than 4000. Life of Pole, vol. i. p. 202.

would

CARDINAL REGINALD POLE.   49

would deliver up POLE into his hands. Upon which the cardinal thus expressed himself: 'The king deceives himself, if he means by this to do me an evil, which will but hasten my repose; he does but offer to disrobe one, who wishes to go to rest.' On the approach of winter, the legate, by the pope's command, returned thro' *Germany* into *Italy*, and came to *Rome*, having left behind him in *Flanders*, and in all the places thro' which he passed, the character of a pious minister of the holy see: on his arrival he made honourable mention of the signal services he had received from the cardinal of *Liege*, to the POPE and the *college of cardinals*, who was afterwards made his holiness's legate in *Flanders* in reward for that service.

THE good cardinal POLE took up his residence in *Rome* for some considerable time, till the pope set out, in the following year 1538, for *Nice* in *Provence*, to be present at an interview with the emperor and the king of *France*, and endeavour to mediate ᵐ a peace between them. He made POLE of
his

ᵐ Neither Father PAUL nor COURAYER, nor the Spanish historian SANDOVAL, will allow the mediating a peace between the emperor and the French king to have been the old pope's motive for so long a journey as from *Rome* to *Nice*. Cardinal QUIRINI calls poor COURAYER *an impudent fellow* for insinuating another cause, though he admits of the authority of a
E   truly

his party on this expedition, with several other cardinals, as one whose presence would grace his train. I remember [n] well, on the first interview between

---

truly impudent one, ARETINE, when he happens to agree with him in opinion.

Diatriba ad Epist. vol. ii. sect. 8. C. Quirini.

P. PAOLO's account of the supposed motive for Paul III's journey to NICE 1538, is in a very few plain, sensible words:

—*In questo medesimo il Pontifice andò a Nizza per intervenire al colloquio del Imperadore & del Rè di Francia, procurato da lui; dando fuori che fosse solamente per metter quei due gran Principi in pace, se bene il fine più principale era di tirar in casa sua il ducato di Milano.*

Istoria del Concil. di Trento, lib. i.

Lord HERBERT relates the same story more at large from the Spanish of SANDOVAL, Fol. p. 499.

Whatever T. PHILIPS says on this interview is not worth considering, as he only gives a verbal translation of Cardinal QUIRINI's words in his Diatriba to the epistles of his 2d vol. sect. 8.

[n] C. QUIRINI and T. PHILIPS lay great weight upon BECCATELLI's testimony as an eye witness of the honour POLE received from CHARLES V. at the interview at NICE. PHILIPS, to make the most of this compliment, draws a very pompous conclusion from it, and to dress up his hero in the finest plumage, sets out with these fine expressions:

" The pope would have the cardinal assist at this negociation, that he might have the advantages of his counsels, and his court be honoured by a person whose reputation was very high through all Europe."

Life of Pole, vol. i. p. 236.

The

CARDINAL REGINALD POLE. 51

between his holiness and the emperor, who came out of the city to do him the honour of a visit to a monastery in the neighbourhood, when the cardinals who attended went forward to meet the emperor, as is the usual ceremony, he bade his chancellor Granville inquire immediately, 'which was 'C. POLE; that he had a great desire to see and 'converse with him; that he well knew the merits 'of his character, and had great personal obli-'gations to him for the zeal he had shewn in the 'cause of his aunt the queen of *England*.' I was present also another time when POLE waited upon the emperor at *Villa Franca* °, who immediately slighted

---

The plain truth is no more than this: PAUL III. had all his principal cardinals about him, and POLE among the rest; the emperor and the king of FRANCE were both very courtly on this occasion, and were very liberal of their complaisance to the whole college of cardinals—BECCATELLI was the panegyrist, and gave every compliment its highest colouring— Let us turn only to his *Life of Contarini*, and we shall find *he* had as many fine speeches bestowed on him at the same place and by the same persons.

° Here it was the emperor kept his court during the interview at NICE (as Beccatelli relates in the *Life of Contarini*) the compliment paid to POLE, he there tells us, was in common with the other: " *gran carezze li fece l' imperatore ch' era* " *allogiato a Villa Franca porto di Nizza.*" He makes the pope also give the same preference to CONTARINI when he embarked on this expedition, as he has here given to POLE:— " *Fra gli altri seco volle che' l* Card. Contarini *andasse, dell* " *opera, & del consiglio del quale si serviva*"—So that upon

E 2 comparing

slighted every other business and engagement, and embraced him with the cordiality of a brother, and honoured him with his conversation for a considerable space of time.

The pope returned before the end of the summer to *Rome*, whither the cardinals Contarini and Pole followed him within a few months, having spent the intermediate time with their friends in *Lombardy* p.

In this interval Paul III. either of his own motion or at the instigation of two crowned heads, projected a second enterprize to take advantage of the present religious feuds in *England*, which were increasing every day; for which purpose the em-

---

comparing these two panegyrics together, both written by the same author, whatever the merits of his patrons were, their common secretary and biographer Beccatelli undoubtedly deserves the praise of a most grateful memorialist.

p C. Quirini and his translator T. Philips, who will never let their hero rest, but pursue him into all his retirements, give us a curious paragraph from an Italian letter written at Priuli's country-seat, from Pole to Contarini, wherein he expresses the general joy on account of the late truce of Nice, by the effect it had on the brains of a poor painter at Verona, who was so affected by it, " che ad ogni parola " parlava delle cose spirituali,"—he did nothing but repeat texts of scripture the whole day—a most wondrous effect on a poor crack-brained painter, and worthy the sage observation of a cardinal!

C. Quirini, vol. ii. ep. 60.

peror

peror and the king of *France* had given him a renewal of their former promise, that they would forbid their subjects all commerce with *England*, which they judged the most effectual means to cause a general insurrection thro' the island; it was agreed also that POLE should be dispatched into the same quarter as before, in quality of legate of the holy see; in consequence of which he entered upon his journey immediately after Christmas 1538.

THAT he might travel with all possible expedition, and run less hazard of falling into the hands of the king of *England*, it was thought adviseable for him to quit his cardinal's habit [1], and take his journey with a small retinue thro' *Spain*, by way of *Toledo*, where the emperor kept his court, and from thence take a circuit by *Guienne* into *France*;

---

[1] We here find POLE abating somewhat of his punctilio and delicacy of character, as he becomes more hackneyed in the trammels of his three masters, the pope, the emperor, and the king of France—He could not possibly submit to lay aside his dress on his first expedition, though after he had been driven from the court of FRANCE and his business was over: " *No* (says T. Philips, vol. i. p. 197) *it was not becoming his character, he did not approve of travelling in disguise;*" but these scruples soon vanished: he now strips himself at the first without a moment's hesitation, and his biographer tells us another story: " *It was agreed upon he should travel in disguise, that his journey might be more secret*—Vol. i. p. 245.

and that as soon as those two princes had fixed the time for laying an embargo on all commerce with *England*, he, in the character of legate, should take up his abode either in *Flanders* or *Picardy*, as seemed most convenient to the plan ʳ concerted. I was one of those who embarked with his *Eminence* on this expedition; we did not reach *Barcelona* till the end of *January*, having been greatly retarded by the severity of the season, and the badness of the roads; the cardinal had 300 miles farther to travel before he could arrive at the Imperial court, and finding his own horses began to fail him, for

---

ʳ Neither C. QUIRINI nor *his translator* T. PHILIPS will allow this second embassy of POLE's to have any treasonable purport in it. " It was all projected (says Quirini, Diatriba " ad Epis. vol. ii. sect. 9.) for the good of HENRY and his " kingdom :"

" Saluti profecto non exitio HENRICI regis, non AN-
" GLIÆ cædibus, sed tranquillitati institutam ipsam
" fuisse—nemini certe licebit in dubium revocare"—

Let me adopt the sensible and ingenious answer of SCHEL-HORN to QUIRINI, as the best reply that can be made to T. PHILIPS, and all other POLE's advocates who have drunk so deep of the *Narcotic cup of bigotry*, as to have all their reasoning and distinguishing faculties rendered useless and insensible, when his actions become the objects of inquiry—" Eo
" scilicet sum ingenio, ut ubi verba factis manifestissime recla-
" mant, verbis etiam speciosissimis omnem plane fidem dene-
" gandam esse censeam—Vox quidem est vox JACOBI, manus
" autem sunt manus ESAVI."

Epis. Schelhornii, vol. i. Quirin. p. 22.

the

the fake of difpatch, he took poft with four attendants, and fet forward with all fpeed for *Toledo*, ordering the reft of his retinue to follow him by eafy ftages. The king of *England* alarmed at his fituation, and doubting what part the emperor would take, having got intelligence of the pope's defigns, fent an ambaffador exprefs to *Toledo*, with offers to enter into an offenfive alliance with Charles immediately againft all his enemies whatfoever. The emperor liftened to his propofals, with a view of diftreffing the king of *France*; and to convince Henry of the fincerity of his intentions, he * paid very little regard to the overtures made him by the cardinal in the pope's

---

* This fecond embaffy of C. Pole's proved as unfuccefsful as the former, in the conduct of which he fhewed himfelf very unable to cope with *the fubtlety of Charles, the addrefs of Francis,* and *the fpirited vigilance of Henry*. His whole behaviour, (upon a fair examination of his own letters, and the Italian memoirs of C. Farnese, who was then at *Toledo*) will appear to have been inadequate, *timid*, and irrefolute;—C. Quirini appears confcious of this failure in his hero, though he has too much *hauteur* in his logic ever to fuffer himfelf to be convinced— A French embaffador, M. de Noailles, who knew him well in his political capacity, has given him the character here drawn of him;

" La faute de la mettre à prompte execution vient de ce
" legat (Polus) qui a, outre ce qui eft *timide & craintif*, fi
" peu de *vertù & d'execution*, qu'il ne fçait qu'un chanfon.
    Lettre de Mr. Noailles, 5me Dec. 1555, tom. iv. Negociations.

name; and when POLE applied to him to fulfil his engagements, he answered, "it was now a very unseasonable time for such an attempt," with other excuses of the like kind; and came at length to a resolution, that POLE should first go and confer with the king of *France*, and he would regulate his own proceedings accordingly. The ‘ cardinal saw plainly whence these exceptions arose, and the artful policy of those two princes, whose aim was, by throwing out such menaces, to bring HENRY into their terms, and strengthen themselves against each other by an alliance with him. The legate thought therefore, that the pursuing his journey into *France* would but confirm the league between the emperor and the king of *England*, and at the same time expose his own person to manifest hazard: he therefore respectfully took his leave of the Imperial court, telling his majesty, "he would "inform his holiness of what had passed, and

---

‘ As fruitless as this extravagant enterprize of POLE's proved to the purposes for which it was avowedly undertaken—*the dethroning of Henry, and restoring the papal power in England*—yet it completed the ruin of his own family, the chief of which were at this time brought to the scaffold for assisting him in a project he was so little able to execute. That they meant *to raise him to the crown* (as T. Philips supposes) is not to be credited; how undeserving he was of such an effort in his favour, his own pusillanimous conduct sufficiently indicated—He stole back to CARPENTRAS to weep over their sufferings, when he should have been hovering over the English coasts with an army at his back, to second them in an attempt, in which he had shamefully involved, and then left them to perish.

"wait

Cardinal REGINALD POLE. 57

" wait for his further instructions." He then took his route backward ᵘ to *Avignon* and *Carpentras*, both which cities are subject to the papal jurisdiction, and neutrals in the present war; from thence he sent dispatches to *Rome*, and a ʷ gentleman

---

ᵘ 'This retreat of the legate POLE back from *Toledo* to *Carpentras*, when he had orders both from the pope and the emperor to proceed on to *France*, betrayed the natural timidity of his temper (maugre all the pains taken both by QUIRINI and PHILIPS to set forth his courage and constancy) insomuch that the cardinal FARNESE, who was then legate extraordinary at the court of *Toledo*, was forced to apologize for his misconduct to the emperor, and confess the true cause of his so speedy retreat, as he acquaints Paul III. in a letter dated Toledo, 21 June 1539.—

—A questo risposi; che certamente V. Sant. quando spaccio il C. Polo da *Roma* li commise che cosi andasse alla Maestà Christianissima comme alla sua, & che poiche SS. Reûma *non per altro che per timor della vita* (sapendo quante insidie le son tese dal Rè d'Inghilterra) si fermo a Carpentras.

Quirini, vol. ii.

How greatly the POPE's whole scheme was embarrassed by this pusillanimous piece of misconduct in POLE, of which the emperor made his advantage, appears in many passages of the four Italian letters written from *Toledo* to the pope by ALESSANDRO FARNESE, and published by C. QUIRINI in his 2d volume, from a MS. in MARCELLUS II.'s family at *Sienna*.

ʷ This person was VINCENT PARPALIA, *Abbe di San Salute*, whom C QUIRINI mistook for POLE's principal associate PRIULI, through his three first volumes, and honoured him as such.—T. PHILIPS, who looked no farther, means also to de

man of his houshold to the court of *France*, where he found the same reserve as to any engagements against *England* as at *Toledo*, HENRY having made the same artful proposals at the same time to both courts, and cajoled the two princes by promising to take part with each of them against the other. The pope sent him orders to stay in those parts where he was: he therefore made choice of *Carpentras* [x], not only as it was more quiet and re-

---

do him honour, by saying, from QUIRINI, "He is men-"tioned by FLAMINIUS, and was of the society of *Viterbo*," vol. i. p. 253. This abbé was indeed an humble retainer of POLE's for many years, and followed him into ENGLAND 1554. He was a very expert negociator, but of more ability than honesty; for he prostituted his services to the French ambassador NOAILLES, betraying to him the secrets of the Imperial and English courts, for which he pleaded poverty, and applied to the constable of *France*, through NOAILLES, for some additional benefice to his poor abbey in SAVOY, in reward for his services.

Ambassade de Noailles, vol. iv. p. 309.

[x] Cardinal QUIRINI and his translator T. PHILIPS give us an extract from an Italian letter of POLE to CONTARINI, to shew how becomingly POLE, PRIULI, and BECCATELLI passed their time in the convent near *Carpentras*, in reading lectures on the book of Psalms—Both POLE and his biographers had certainly forgot that he was not there in the character nor even the habit of a cardinal, which he had laid aside for the purposes of the negotiation he had undertaken—It was therefore very much out of place to be reading theological discourses in a convent, when he should have been acting the vigilant emissary at the court of *Paris*, in prosecution of the plan he had at first engaged in.

tired

tired than *Avignon*, but chiefly as it was the residence of *Sadolet*, his very intimate friend and brother cardinal, in the social enjoyment of whose many amiable qualities he promised himself much gratification. Here he spent six months, to the mutual [y] happiness of himself and his friends. On his recall to *Rome*, he passed, by way of *Marseilles* and *Nice*, thro' *Piedmont*, and came to *Verona*, where he spent some time with M. Giberti, bishop of that see, who had been a very serviceable friend and companion to him on his former embassy. At the close of the year 1539 he returned to *Rome*, when the pope, who had a great sense of his late services, and knew the dangers he would be exposed to from the insidious attempts of Henry VIII. in so populous a place as *Rome*, appointed him a guard for the defence of his person, and

---

[y] *Con molto contento suo*, says Beccatelli; but he who was of his company, must have known how greatly that happiness of Pole's was allayed by the continual dread he had upon him, lest the pope, by the instigation of the emperor, and at the further instance of the Card. Farnese, should insist on his prosecuting his first projected embassy into *France*. He expresses his great anxiety on this occasion to his friend Contarini, in an Italian letter from that very place—

— certo Io sono forte perplesso, & piu desidero di quiete che altro—Questa sospensione d'animo fra le altre cose mi fa anche meno godere questa quiete, e questa dolcissima compagnia—Lettera 79. vol. ii. C. Quirini.

conferred

conferred on him afterwards the dignity of *Legate of Viterbo*, a government of ease and leisure, which he enjoyed for many years.

In the beginning of the year 1542, Paul III. being desirous, if possible, to root out heresy, and bring all Christendom into an union with the Romish church, proclaimed a council to be held at *Trent*, to which he sent three [z] cardinals of note to preside as legates of the holy see; Cardinal Parisio, an eminent Canonist; Cardinal Morone, whom he had lately promoted to the purple for the zeal he had distinguished himself by at the diet of *Spires*; and the third was cardinal Pole, whose learning, discretion, and courtesy of temper were well known to him, and who was besides a particular favourite of the powers north of *Italy*.

These [a] deputies repaired to *Trent*; but on account of the fresh troubles which broke out in *Germany*,

---

[z] Beccatelli speaks very cursorily of this first abortive convention at *Trent*, and therefore does not attend to strict accuracy in point of time; when he says, "*sopravenuto il* 1542," for the pope's bull was not published till *May* 22, to appoint the meeting the 1*st of November*, and the cardinal legates were not dispatched thither till the 26 *of August*.
P. Paolo, lib. 1.

[a] Father Paul accounts for the pope's choice of his three deputies in words to this effect:
"Parisio,

Germany, and other parts, between the Christian princes, they could not open the council, so that within a few months they returned to *Rome*; from whence POLE, after a few days stay in that city, retired to the enjoyment of that learned leisure he found in his legateship of *Viterbo* [b]; between which place

---

" PARISIO, for his skill in the canon law; MORONE for
" his address in business; and POLE, that *England* might not
" want a representative, although HENRY had withdrawn his
" subjection to the see of *Rome*." Libro 1mo.

Yet, notwithstanding all this parade, their convention was ineffectual and their prorogation disgraceful—Pole himself confesses in a letter to the POPE—*Ægrius ferebam superiorum mensium ignominiam.*—Vol. iv. Epist. 17.

[b] T. PHILIPS, studious of making his hero appear in the character of a man of business and activity, which was ever foreign to his province, even subverts the very nature of the government of *Viterbo*, and talks *of his vigilance in his administration there*, as pompously as if he had been governor of all the German provinces; whereas BECCATELLI always describes this post given him by PAUL III. as *governo piacevole & d'otio* " a pleasant retirement where he had nothing to do,"— *otio de studii suoi*—" a retreat for learned leisure;" best suited both to the talents and the temper of the master of it.

The *pious indolence* to which the gentle cardinal and his favourite devotée the marchioness of *Pescara* resigned themselves in those sweet solitudes, seemed to breathe much of the mystic spirit of *Quietism* which infected the elegant mansions of *St. Cyr* in 1687. We see in the legate of *Viterbo* the same *romantic theology* that afterwards captivated the Abbé DE FENELON; and the religious reveries of Madame GUION are but a faint copy

place and *Rome* he divided his time with much credit and reputation till the year 1545, when Pope PAUL, seeing cause to hope the state of Christendom was now in a more favourable disposition for such an enterprize, began to deliberate a second time on summoning a council to meet at *Trent*, to which he deputed three legates, the cardinals DE MONTE, SANTA CROCE, and POLE. Many bishops assembled thither from *Italy*, *France*, *Spain*, and other countries; and upon opening the council they debated many material points with great harmony and unanimity. This temper peculiarly distinguished the three legates, whom I attended as secretary for many months, and was a witness of the great distinction paid to POLE by all present. He had the misfortune to have a rheumatic [c] disorder fall into one of his arms, owing to the

---

copy of the devout raptures of the Italian marchioness, whom the pious cardinal with the same passionate enthusiasm adopted for his mother, as Madame GUION used to boast of her disciple the Abbé Fenelon for her son.

Card. Polus Marchionissæ Piscariæ, vol. iii. epis. 46. Quirini; & M. Voltaire du Quietisme.

[c] Of this rheumatic defluxion (which T. PHILIPS calls a *catarrh* in his arm) it may be said in the words of JUVENAL:

Provida POMPEIO dederat CAMPANIA *febres*
Optandas—

Whether POL's sickness was pretended, is needless to argue; it is demonstration, his collegues thought him too hasty in quitting

the coldness of the season, and the sharp air of that place; his complaint not growing better he was advised

---

quitting TRENT, and imputed it to some shyness on the *Article of Justification*.

Cardinal Santa Croce writes thus to MAFFEI, 25 June 1546:

> "Cardinal POLE, I find, designs to set out immediately for *Treville*, having got the pope's leave: *But we, though we have not less occasion than himself for a little respite and change of air, are resolved nevertheless to attend the debate on the article of Justification.*"
>
> Translation of part of an Italian letter, from the *Minutes* of what passed at Trent in 1545 and 1546—being C. Santa Croce's own register found in a MS. of his Family's. Quirini, vol. iv. p. 277.

To explain this point more fully, from an examination of the Italian letters, and minutes of the proceedings at Trent, published in four vol. Quirini.—*The Article of Justification* came on in the council 21 June 1546. The Card. SANTA CROCE tells MAFFEI on the 25th, that POLE was setting out *presto* for *Treville*, where we find him, by his own letter to his collegues, July the 1st—On the 30th of June they write to him for his opinion on that question, which he waves answering, for three reasons, "*per rispetto dell' absentia, insufficientia, & indispositione*, and desires them to communicate their future commands *viva voce* by the bishop of *Worcester*.—On the 26th of September the bishop of *Worcester* had either brought or sent POLE a copy of the decree, according to his own desire; he then excuses himself a second time, "*non li essendo concesso d'interrogare, & d'esser instrutto di molte cose, oltre che sono sì gravato dalla mia indispositione che sono mal atto a pensar* (non che a scriver) *in materia di questa importanza.*" He then promises.

advised to go to *Padua*, where he might consult some able physicians, and have the benefit of a softer climate; this advice he followed, and in a few months after the council was adjourned to *Bologna*[d], upon suspicion of the plague breaking out at

---

promises, after so much importunity, to send his opinion *viva voce* in a few days, which he does 18 Oct. 1546. by one Dr. MORIGLIA, *suo familiare*.

These *letters* seem fully to refute the notion T. PHILLIPS has taken up, of supposing the decree on that article to have been finally drawn up, and finished as it passed the council, by POLE (on account of a transcript of it being found among his papers and published by H. PENING) since it appears *he would never once write his opinion* upon that article, though expresly solicited so to do, but only gave his sentiments upon it *viva voce* by MORIGLIA.

Lettere Italiene, 184, & seq. Quirini, vol. iv. Philips's Life of Pole, vol. i. p. 369.

There are many more passages (among the XXXII *Italian Letters* published from a MS of C.S. CROCE's by QUIRINI) which discover an earnestness in the two other legates for POLE's return to *Trent*, and a displeasure at his protracted stay; and a peevishness in him on their frequent remonstrances; as well as an unwillingness to return again to the council (see the IX, XVI, XIX, XXIII).

[d] The suspicion of a plague was the alleged pretence, but the real cause for adjourning the council to *Bologna*, was, " The POPE began to grow jealous that the bishops were too " busy with his power, and might retrench somewhat from " it:

" Resto

CARDINAL REGINALD POLE.

at *Trent*, and soon after prorogued: so that the cardinal, on the recovery of his health, had the pope's leave to go back to *Rome*, his holiness being very desirous of having him near him, as he had experienced the usefulness of his pen in settling many nice points of doctrine or discipline with the Christian princes, most of the papers on these subjects being consigned to the management of C. POLE: of this nature was *The Brief* which the pope sent to the emperor on his publication of the *Interim*[*]; as also *The Answer to* DON DIEGO HURTADO,

---

" *Restò pieno di sospetto* (says Father PAUL) *che il concilio non partorisse qualche gran mostruosità a prejudicio di Lui, & dell' autorità Pontificia.*" Libro 2do.

He therefore chose to bring them within his reach: this shameful scheme so enraged the emperor, that he so far forgot his reverence to the triple crown, as to threaten to throw cardinal S. CROCE into the river *Adice* if he attempted to adjourn it.

Father PAUL and Lord HERBERT.

[*] CHARLES V. with a bold spirit of indignation at the religious intrigues of the court of *Rome*, took upon him to publish *a Formulary of Faith and Discipline*, till a plan should be settled by a general council: the history of the INTERIM (as it was called) is given at large by F. PAUL, lib. iii.; but it does not appear from any authority but BECCATELLI's, that C. POLE had a hand in any of the pieces that were thrown out against this imperial edict; neither does it appear that the pope published any *brief* against it at all. Father PAUL says only,

F " The

TADO, *the Imperial Minister's Protest* [f] at the court of *Rome*, which was thought to be drawn up with great judgment, and much commended. The cardinal was very *adroit* on these occasions, having acquired, when very young, an easy and elegant style in his Latin compositions, and being also very diligent in selecting his materials, and very nice and exact in the arrangement of them.

He spent his time in the manner I have thus related till the death of Paul III. which happened after a few days illness, in November 1549.

The cardinals assembled at the usual time in a very numerous body, to the election of a new

---

" The sharp-sighted old pope found the emperor had over-
" shot himself; that by thus engaging with all parties, he
" would bring them all upon him ; *that there would be no occa-*
" *sion for him to interfere, as it would be more for the interest*
" *of the holy see to have it published than not,*" 4to, p. 298.—
He seems therefore to have avoided writing against it, and only sent orders to C. Sfondrato *to make some little opposition to it,* and withdraw at the time of its promulgation.

[f] C. Quirini has published a copy of this *Answer*, vol. iv. p. 382. on which some remarks will be found at the close of this book, among the observations on *Pole's Writings*.

T. Philips calls Pole's writing these two pieces (if he did so) " his being the chief defence of the council for the three
" following years after he left *Trent*." vol. i .p. 381.

pope;

pope ; and Cardinal FARNESE, who had great weight in the conclave, deliberating with himself what person he should patronize on this occasion, who might make a respectable successor to his grandfather, and a serviceable friend to himself, he pitched upon C. POLE ; in which he was seconded by many of the electors, especially of the *Imperial* faction, who knew how high he stood in their master's favour: the *French* party, who were at that time at variance with the *Imperialists*, set themselves to oppose his election, thro' fear of his too great attachment ‡ to the emperor's interests, in which they persuaded the king their master to be of the same opinion ; some other electors sided

---

‡ The conduct of the conclave (in which C. DI MONTE was elected pope, and C. POLE set aside) is differently related by other writers not so much devoted to his person and interest as BECCATELLI, or T. PHILIPS, who copies his relation of this election from him.

GRATIANI, a great admirer of POLE, his cotemporary, (and as PHILIPS characterises him in his *Preface*, " one of the best " judges of men and manners) tells a somewhat different tale:

" The IMPERIAL faction (he says) would have elected
" POLE for his zeal to their master; the *French* opposed him
" for that very reason. There was a day wherein he would
" have been chosen, if they could have procured him *one*
" vote, but neither *awe* nor *authority* could prevail on *one* to
" second FARNESE's motion; so that the time elapsed, the
" French party came in the next day, and he had no further
" prospect."
Gratiani de Casibus Illust. Viror. p. 220.

with the *French* party in hopes of promoting their own success, yet the majority was so strong in his favour, that the opponents to C. FARNESE's [a] motion began to despair of frustrating his proposal. All the cardinals who were present in the conclave, which lasted more than two months, can witness one very remarkable circumstance to POLE's honour, that neither he, nor any of his friends [1], ever canvassed one single person in his behalf, during the whole progress of the election, which seemed to incline so much in his favour; neither did he himself betray the least symptom of anxiety upon the occasion, but preserved his usual chear-

---

[a] The *Conclave de Pontifici*, published in 1657 (which professes to relate the proceedings at the several papal elections as they really were) gives two reasons for POLE's failure; the first very opposite to this account of BECCATELLI's—

1. Perche il C. FARNESE (whom PHILIPS sometimes calls BORGHESE sometimes FARNESIUS) tacitamente piegave alla parte *Francese*:

2. Perche i CARDINALI vecchi ricevano injuria di vedersi anteposto a quella dignità il C. POLO, & questo fù la causa che molti di loro s'opposero.
       Istoria del Conclave di Giulio Terzo.

[1] As this assertion,—that none of POLE's friends even canvassed one person for him,—is point-blank contradictory to GRATIANI's words quoted in the preceding note, who says, *neque metus neque authoritas quenquam permovit* to give him even *one* vote: I shall leave it to T. Philips, on a future occasion, to settle the point between these two friends of POLE, and suspend my own belief.

              fulness

fulness the whole time; and if any of the electors, as they often did, said to him, "My lord, the "choice will certainly be in your favour." His answer was, "I beseech you to forego all partia- "lity, and consider only the interest of the holy "see; vote as the Spirit * of God shall direct you, "and let his influence only be your guide." He followed his studies and devotions the whole time, as if he had been in his own private apartment, as *The Treatises* [1] he then composed can witness, which I shall mention at the close of this history.

THE

---

* There is so much of that *affected self-denial* (which was the ruling maxim of a very bad man in the annals of our country) in this behaviour of POLE, that one can scarce admit it to be the criterion of a good man: the admirers of the cardinal must pardon me therefore for drawing a parallel, in this single circumstance of his history, between him and the *Protector* CROMWELL.

When a committee was held to advise with him upon accepting the title of king, CROMWELL told them, "He would "*seek the Lord* for counsel, and then declare his resolution."

POLE desires his friends, who would have promoted him to the popedom, *to seek the Lord* before they declared their sentiments in his favour—And both of them, notwithstanding this specious hypocrisy, would have accepted their crowns with joy if *human means* could have effected their wishes.

[1] *One* treatise Pole wrote during the conclave, which BECCATELLI does not mention, but GRATIANI has recorded to POLE's *immortal ridicule*: "He was so certain of his own "success,

The Spanish cardinal of St. James remarked, that one morning, upon making the *scrutiny* in the chapel, wherein there were but two votes wanting to carry the election in Pole's favour, he fixed his eyes upon him as they stood all together, to mark what effect it would have upon him; but was surprized to observe the steadiness with which he received it, without the least alteration from his wonted calmness. Another day, when some of the conclave reflected on him for being ambitious of the popedom before his time, he answered, "It was an object of dread, not of ambition, and he should pity the man who looked on it in any other light." He shewed the same firmness of temper on two very trying occasions; the one, in not being elevated by the prospect of a dignity he had so much reason to expect, the other in not being depressed by the calumnies that were cast upon him to depreciate his character; some aspersing him as a heretic [m], and for neglect of duty

in

"success, that he wrote an oration in the conclave, to return his thanks to the cardinals for the honour they did him in choosing him, which composition is reported to have been seen by many persons."

Gratiani de Casibus Illust. Viror. 219.

[m] Most of the historians, who mention the strong contest for the popedom on the death of Paul III. hint the objection of heresy brought against Pole by one or more members of the conclave, and the immediate turn it gave to the election.

F. Paul

Cardinal REGINALD POLE.

in his legatine office at *Viterbo*, where he had exercised too little rigour againſt offenders; that he had alſo a natural daughter [a], whom he had ſe-

---

F. Paul ſays the objection was made by his own friend and principal intimate, before he became legate of *Viterbo*, Caraffa, the *Theatine Cardinal*.

"Oppugnandolo il C. Theatino, che foſſe macchiato delle opinioni *Lutherane*, fece ritirar molti." Lib. 320.

The author of the *Conclave di Giulio Terzo* ſays,

"Era di parte di *Franceſi* il C. Turone, huomo molto religioſo & exemplare di vita, il quale, intendendo il trattato fatto in favor di C. Pole, l'accuſo publicamente d'*hereſia*, & che per queſta ſola cauſa, come maggior di tutto, non doveva eſſer eletto." 4to, p. 127.

Both theſe objectors were men of very ſtrict morals, and very ſcrupulous in their religious conduct; and Caraffa's diſſenſions with Pole were many years ſubſequent to this accuſation, ſo that he could not then be ſaid to be biaſſed by prejudice.

[a] Archbiſhop Parker, who was Pole's ſucceſſor in the ſee of Canterbury, and ſeems to have had more tenderneſs for *his* fame than *he* had for Cranmer's, ſays,

"The ſcandal of Pole's intimacy with an abbeſs in the neighbourhood of *Viterbo*, was the common ſubject of the *Paſquins* at *Rome* at that time." Antiquitates Brit. p. 519.

In juſtice to his memory I muſt obſerve, that this imputation on his character is not mentioned by the author of the *Conclave di Pontifici*, though *his hereſy, his too early ambition*, and *his ſlaviſh attachment to the emperor*, are much inſiſted on.

erected in a convent at *Rome*. These reflections were cast upon him by his competitors for the triple crown; to which his answer was, " when these accusations should be alleged against him in due form, and his accusers confronted with him, he would make his defence in such a manner that the truth should appear beyond contradiction; tho' the charge against him was of such a nature, that it confuted itself, since many persons could testify what fatigues he had undergone, to the frequent hazard of his life, out of zeal for the holy see, beside the sufferings of his nearest relations; that ° he had lost a mother and an elder brother, who fell victims to the resentment of that bloody tyrant the king of *England*, for holding the same religious opinions with himself, whose crime was

---

° POLE's pathetic appeal to the ashes of his nearest relations (whose death he had hastened through his zealous attachment to the Romish faith) was no convincing reply to the THEATINE cardinal's accusation of heresy: this charge was, for behaviour subsequent to those events; Caraffa was one of the chief persons who encouraged Pole to go to *Rome* on the summons of PAUL III. (Quirini, vol. i. epist. 45.) though he knew and acknowleged it was to the hazard of the lives and fortunes of his family in *England*. POLE's resolution on that occasion he therefore well knew and applauded. The heresy he now reproached him with, was a blemish of a later date, contracted within the walls of *Viterbo*, which (notwithstanding C. Quirini's elaborate but unargumentative vindication, in 50 pages of his 3d vol.) was, not injuriously, supposed to have been *a sanctuary, if not a seminary, for Lutherans*.

his

his opposition to the heretical tenets of HENRY, who courted his compliance with the offer of the first dignities in his kingdom. With regard to his conduct at *Viterbo*, if the people under his care were so well disposed as not to deserve any severities, he ought not therefore to be accused of negligence, as Providence had given a blessing to his government, that should be acknowledged with gratitude, of which the people themselves were sufficient witnesses." The reproach of his having a daughter will be confuted by the fact itself, without any endeavours of his own to set it right, since the first inventors of that calumny had made it their business to inquire, who that young person was whom the cardinal had sent to be educated in the nunnery, and had found to their disappointment, that she was an unhappy orphan, the daughter of an *English* lady deceased, whom the cardinal had taken under his protection to save her from being abandoned; nay more, he had given orders for the depositing of 100 crowns, in a *bank* p established for such charities, for her use,

---

p This charitable fund, for raising interest upon small sums for the benefit of poor orphans, is called by BECCATELLI *Il Monte della Fede.* An institution of a similar kind was founded in the same century 1584, by pope Gregory XIII. which still subsists, by the name of *Il sacro Monte della Pietà*, " where " they both lend money upon small pledges to poor families, " without interest, and also pay interest for any small sums " which industrious people deposit there for security."
Il Mercurio Errante dà Rossini, p. 82.

over

over and above what her mother had left behind her; that the capital and accumulating interest might hereafter be a sufficient portion for her in marriage: this was one of his silent acts of beneficence, which he performed without founding his own praises.

THE [q] cardinals, who were members of the conclave, can witness the truth of another incident; that one night C. FARNESE had prevailed on a competent number of the electors to have carried the election for POLE by *adoration* [r], if he would have

given

---

[q] BECCATELLI dwells very tediously upon the cabals of the conclave, though he deserves indeed the honour of a very zealous assertor of his master's reputation; but (if Gratiani says true) neither the merits or demerits of the candidates can possibly influence their election: " *The Holy Spirit* determines the
" whole matter, sometimes by fixing on a bad one to scourge
" mankind for their offences against God; sometimes inclining
" their choice to a good man, to preserve them in their duty,
" and in a proper observance of true piety and religion."
Gratiani, p. 219.

Thus will zealous ROMANISTS, rather than disavow the *inspiration of their conclaves*, adjudge the Spirit of God to be the author of evil; and the most shameless intrigues that can disgrace the worst of men, shall be ascribed to the immediate influence of the Holy Ghost.

[r] " There are three ways by which popes are chosen, by *scru-*
" *tiny*, *access*, or *adoration*. The first method is, when every
" cardinal writes on a scroll of paper the name of that person
" whom he designs to be elected, &c.—If the choice is not de-
" termined

given his consent to it; but he objected, "that it
"ought to be done in a regular and canonical manner,
"in the morning, at the hour of *mass*, and not in the
"darkness of the night*, which might carry the
"appearance of stealth; and if it was the pleasure
"of God to place him in the papal chair, he
"would doubtless effect it in the morning as well

"termined by *scrutiny*, it is then tried by *access*, which is per-
"formed thus: All the cardinals sitting in their places, one
"arises, and goes to the person he designs to have elected, and
"says, *Ego accedo ad Rev' Dom'* &c. The third way, by
"*adoration*, is performed almost in the same manner as that by
"*access*. The cardinal approaching him whom he desires to
"have elected pope, with a profound reverence, and lowly
"bowing."
Sir Paul Rycault's Introduction to his Continuation of
Platina.

PHILIPS takes his whole account of the papal election from this work (vol. i. p. 450.) except that he calls the third method *acclamation*, and not *adoration*.

* POLE's extraordinary nicety in rejecting an election in his favour made *in the night*, reflected on that of his great friend and patron the late pope PAUL III. who was chosen in an uncanonical hour.

"*La notte* fù creato papa di comun volere, et consenso il
"medesimo C. Farnese."
Conclavo del Paolo 3zo.

This very election also in favour of JULIUS III. was determined *in the night*; and the history of the conclaves will furnish us with so many examples of the same kind, as render Pole's scruples very particular.

"as

76 THE LIFE OF

" as then," and he refused *to be adored. A most extraordinary instance of denial not easily to be parallel'd!*

ON the morrow the electors changed their opinions for some of the reasons [t] I have before alleged. I cannot here pass by another story, in testimony of his unconcernedness; one of the cardinals (who was obliged to leave the conclave on account of sickness, and who was no friend of POLE's) being asked by one of his acquaintance, what would be the event of the election? and what he thought of the English cardinal? replied, " they cannot possibly make choice of a more un- " fit person for pope, for he was *a mere log of* " *wood*; since neither the prospect of success, nor " the artifices practised to supplant him, had the " least effect upon him." Wondrous! that he should esteem him no better than a *statue*, for what he ought rather to have pronounced him somewhat *angelical* [u].

IT

---

[t] Some other popular reasons are alleged in the *Conclave del P. Paolo* III. for setting POLE aside.

' His being born in a country of hereticks—his leaning to ' their opinions himself—his incompetent age, &c. &c.'

[u] This compliment upon Pole's *marvelous composedness* is work'd up into the most extravagant Hyperbole of Italian panegyric, in which BECCATELLI has taken a flight beyond the reach of

DUDI-

It happened afterwards in the course of the election, that Cardinal MORONE was proposed by the *Imperialists* (as they were called who voted in opposition to the French faction.) He was but forty-one years old, but thro' his extraordinary merits was thought worthy of that dignity; when they came to the *scrutiny*, MORONE had 26 votes of the Imperial party, and two of the *French*, so that he wanted but two votes * to secure his election. POLE was greatly pleased at this, being better satisfied to see a man equal to the character in St. PETER's chair, than to have filled it himself. But MORONE, thanking his friends for the honour they designed him, would not consent to a second scrutiny in his favour; but begged they would resume their first proposal, and confer the papacy on POLE: which appearing now impracticable through the prevalence of the *French* faction, POLE conjured them

---

DUDITHIUS, GRATIANI, or even T. PHILPPS. What was the cardinal's opinion of himself on this behaviour will be seen when we come to speak of his letter to the *Spanish* bishop, FRANCISCO DE NAVARA.

* BECCATELLI's account of the election is here imperfect, as he does not mention how may cardinals were present in the conclave; whereas, if 30 votes, as he says, would have sufficed to have made Morone's a legal majority, the number of cardinals present must have been 44; because 'by a constitution 'of *Alexander* III. he only was to be deemed canonically 'elected, who obtained his choice by more than two thirds of 'the college of cardinals present.' (S. Paul Rycault.)

to turn their thoughts on some other person; upon which the cardinals FARNESE and DE GUISE, who were the leaders in the conclave, determined at last to make the election [x] in favour of the Cardinal DI MONTE, who took the name of JULIUS III. and to lose no time, it was resolved to carry it into execution the same night. C. FARNESE prevailed with POLE to submit to DI MONTE's being elected, to which he assured him, he not only readily consented, but would also be present at the confirma-

---

[x] There is an interruption in the history of POLE's life for three years, from the conclusion of JULIUS III's election in 1550 to the discovery of him among the *Benedictine* monks at *Maguxa*, by a letter to the *Doge of Venice*, written 5 July 1553. This interval C. QUIRINI supposes him to have spent between *Rome* and *Viterbo*, ' very busy in assisting the pope in the ar-' duous affairs of the church.' (vol. iv. appar. XLVI.) T. PHILIPS also, for want of *documents*, as he calls them, very peaceably acquiesces in Quirini's supposal (vol. i. p. 460.) We find him indeed at *Rome* in *June* 1550, writing that very extraordinary apology for his conduct in the late conclave to F. DE NAVARRA; but ' had he been held in such considera-' tion by the Pontif JULIUS III.' as T. PHILIPS supposes, Why did not we see him again at the council of *Trent* in 1551? Had the late feuds of the conclave been forgotten, or POLE been of high estimation with the present pope, he who presided, as PHILIPS tells us, with so much credit in the two former councils, would not now have been set aside; but the truth was, HENRY VIII. was now dead, and Pole's merits at the court of *Rome* expired with him; or Cardinal DI MONTE had seen somewhat in his conduct when he was his colleague at *Trent*, which caused him to overlook him when he became JULIUS III.

tion

tion of it: whereupon they assembled in the chapel, and performed their *adoration* in form to the new pope about ten o' clock at night. When Cardinal POLE presented himself to kiss his holiness's feet among the rest, the pope raised him up and embraced him, with tears in his eyes, as the person who had, as it were, bequeathed him the popedom, since he had, thro' a scruple in point of rectitude, suffered it to pass by himself. This was a circumstance he often mentioned afterwards, and when he found himself engaged in a war with *France* on account of *Mirandola*, and greatly chagrined by the troubles he was brought into, in discourse one day with the Cardinal ST. ANGELO, he reproached himself, saying, ' he knew not ' what offence he had been guilty of to bring upon ' him this visitation, unless it was the opposing so ' upright a candidate as Cardinal POLE.'

WHEN the conclave broke up, POLE retired with the same calmness with which he had entered, convinced in his own mind, that he had rather escaped a weighty burden, than been deprived of an acquisition of honour: ' Peradventure (he said) ' I was not a sufficient instrument to effect the good ' purposes which Providence has designed to work ' under the present pontificate.' He also consoled several of his own principal opponents, who bore their disappointments with less composure than himself. In fine his whole conduct, in the judgment of all wise and good men, was highly meritorious.

There

There is yet extant a *Latin Epistle* [7] of his, in the true

---

[7] This very curious letter of C. Pole's, written to his friend, the *Spanish* bishop, at *Trent*, from his retreat at *Bagnarea*, a few months after the breaking up of the conclave wherein he had been unsuccessful, must have been either printed or handed about in MS. as a very remarkable composition in the time our author wrote, since he speaks of it as a performance well known to the world. C. Quirini has published it with the rest of Pole's letters; but, with due deference to Beccatelli and all others its admirers, I must beg leave to declare, that it seems to me *so wonderous a piece of fanaticism*, that after reading it over many times, and striving to discover its particular beauties, I cannot think of it otherwise than as the letter of a madman.

He says, "He was verily persuaded in himself, that God had transformed him into *an ass*; hanc jumenti personam mihi a Deo impositam fuisse," which rendered him insensible alike to the reproaches of his enemies, and the encouragement of his friends—"That when two cardinals came to his cell, which stood near the door of the chapel, into which they would have persuaded him to let them lead him; that they might elect him that very night, *by adoration*; he immediately fansied himself *the ass*, which was tied to his master's door, which Christ sent two of his disciples to loosen and lead away, that he might ride on it into *Jerusalem*; he therefore submitted at first, after some little reluctance; but recollecting that Christ rode into *Jerusalem* in broad day-light, and not at night, he intreated they would do the like by him—"If (says he) it happened afterwards that Christ did not use me, to make his entry into the holy city (i. e. the church) it is no proof that I was not at that time *in the form of an ass*, but that God had no occasion for me for that purpose," &c. &c.

It

true spirit of Christian resignation, which he wrote to F. DI NAVARA, a *Spanish* bishop, in answer to a consolatory letter from him on his supposed disappointment.

WHEN *Julius* III. was established in the papal see, and the war began to break out the ensuing year in *Lombardy* against the *French*, with the siege of *Mirandola*, insomuch that *Rome* itself was disturbed by these commotions, C. POLE, who disrelished such tumults, began to think of retiring, with the pope's permission, out of that city to some place of tranquillity; and being *Cardinal Protector of the Benedictine Order*, and much caressed by the brethren of *Monte Cassino* [*], he chose for his retreat

---

It consists of 12 pages in quarto, of such ridiculous stuff as what I have here quoted, and seems (spite of the encomiums given it by BECCATELLI, DUDITHIUS, QUIRINI, and T. PHILIPS) to be such a *masterpiece of enthusiasm*, as a friend must lament to read, and an indifferent person must laugh at.
Quirini, vol. iv. epist. 29.

[*] POLE succeeded CONTARINI in this character (see Vita del C. Contarini, sect. 27.) The *Benedictines* had the name here given them by their first founder, who erected his first monastery at *Monte Cassino*, though he met with great opposition from the evil spirit (as St. GREGORY relates in his dialogues) before he could accomplish his work; he was buried on that chosen spot; and his order became afterwards in such *wondrous* repute, that in the time of pope JOHN XXII. (above 400 years ago) there were computed above *forty thousand saints* of that society only.
Supplement to Dugdale, vol. ii.

a convent of theirs at *Maguzano*, in the *Veronese*, upon the *Lago di Garda*, a very healthy and solitary spot; in which the pope readily indulged him. Thither he retired [a] with his whole family, and spent several months in that favourite society to his intire satisfaction.

During his abode there, Edward VI. [b] king of *England*, died, and so suddenly, that many imputed

---

[a] Hither Pole retired (as Quirini tells us first, and then *his echo* T. Philips) to bewail the loss of his deceased friends Bembo, Contarini, Sadolet, Giberti, and above all the marchioness of Pescara; but Gratiani gives the more probable reason ("as great an advocate as he was of Pole's, and "one of the best judges, in T. Philips's opinion, of men and "manners") when, after speaking of his defeat in the contest for the popedom, he says,

"Polus, ut post tam insignem repulsam, quam tamen animo æquabili & constanti tulit, hominum sermones oculosque "vitaret, secessit urbe, abdiditque se monasterio, quod est ad "ripam *Benaci* lacûs, inter *Brixiam* ac *Veronam*, cui nomen "*Magazano*."
Gratiani de Casibus Illust. Vir. p. 220.

[b] The untimely death of this young *protestant prince* was so great a matter of triumph and exultation to the *Romanists*, that pope Julius, as soon as he heard the news, struck a medal at *Rome*, charged with *his own figure, bearing the triple crown* on one side, and on the reverse, this *inscription*,

Gens, & regnum quod non servierit tibi, peribit.
M. Bayle.

puted his death to the evil designs of the duke of *Northumberland*, who aspired to the throne; but the princess MARY, sister of the late king, and the undoubted heir to the crown, having *miraculously* defeated the *Northumberland* party, and brought the duke to the scaffold, revived the catholic worship again in ENGLAND. Whereupon Pope JULIUS, to forward so good a work, immediately appointed POLE *apostolic legate* to that kingdom, and investing him with full powers to enter upon his office, gave him orders to leave his monastic retreat, and transport himself with all speed into FLANDERS.

THE cardinal, zealous for the glory of the church, and of his own native country, set forward ᶜ the October following, and came to *Di-*

In the same insolent style is the letter written in the pope's name to C. POLE on the first news of that event; it begins,

A Questi Giorni s'intese la morte di *Quel Giovane Chi era chiamato il Rè d'Inghilterra.*
Quirini, vol. iv. Lettᵃ 39.

ᶜ BECCATELLI (though he never fails to strew flowers in his hero's way where-ever he attends him) has been very superficial in his narration of POLE's expedition from *Magazano* into *Flanders*, and of the several checks and impediments he met with on his way—DUDITHIUS has been enabled from the information of BAPTISTO BINARDI (who revised and enlarged his work, from many materials his attendance on POLE had supplied him with) to be much more diffuse and particular in his account of this journey, from whom T. PHILIPS has transcribed it into his second volume, p. 29, &c.

Ilingben, to a monastery belonging to the cardinal of *Augsberg*, who waited for him there, and received him with great politeness on his arrival. After a few days stay, he was desirous of pursuing his journey into *Flanders*, notwithstanding the severity of the winter-season, had not DON JUAN DE MENDOZA been dispatched from the emperor, who kept his court at BRUSSELS, with credentials from him to signify his Imperial majesty's desire, that he would not proceed any farther for the present, but halt at *Dilingben* or *Liege*, which-ever he chose; the particular reasons for which delay should be explained to him at a proper opportunity. The cardinal thought it expedient not to dispute [d] the point, and disoblige the emperor. He therefore

---

[d] CHARLES V. although he was so much courted by the see of *Rome*, and flattered with the title of the Great *Constantine* of the council of *Trent*, had too much of the sagacity and spirit of a prince, not to discern and despise the artful falshood of that church and court; the first he ever treated with disregard, and the latter with contempt: neither did he spare cardinals or popes, if they crossed his humour too abruptly. He had a very strong temptation to have carried CLEMENT VII. prisoner to *Madrid*, for not being more supple under his confinement at *St. Angelo*—He threatened to throw C. CERVINI into the *Adice* for presuming to adjourn the council from *Trent* to *Bologna*—And he snubbed C. POLE so sorely for coming down into *Flanders* contrary to his orders, that he complains to C. MORONE. "He was afraid he would cudgel him with "his batoon, and drive him to his monastery at *Maguzano*."

Se

therefore stopped at *Dilingben*, and sent advice to ROME * of what had happened. The emperor's motive for this detainer, as it appeared afterwards, was, that being at that time in treaty for a match between his son PHILIP and the QUEEN OF ENGLAND, he was apprehensive that the *English*, who did not approve of that alliance, might declare openly against it, and set up POLE at the head of their party, who was a favourite among them, and much in the good graces ᶜ of the queen herself.

Se V. S. Reverendissima pensarà sopra le parole che mi disse prima sua Maestà in proposito del mio ritorno; vederà che se non voleva pigliar in mano il Bastone, & cacciarmi, non mi poteva far maggior violentia con parole.
Quirini, vol. iv. Lett. 51.

ᵃ POLE gave great offence to pope JULIUS by the advices he sent to *Rome*, being so intimidated by the check he had received from the emperor, that *his zeal for the church and his native country* (so much gloried in by Beccatelli) forsook him in an instant, and he was for flying back to his Benedictine brethren. Card. MORONE was ordered to acquaint him with the pope's displeasure, and from POLE's vindication (which consists of a most prolix letter in Italian of 14 or 15 pages) we learn, that the charge against him was (Quirini, vol. iv. l. 50.)

Mostrandolo sospetto che per satietà delle cose del mondo, Io piglio volontiere ogni occasione di ritirarmi dai negotii—

So *short* a charge, that needed so *long* an exculpation, could not be very ill grounded—

ᶜ The visionary idolaters of POLE, when he was disappointed of the triple crown, would fain have flattered him with the hope of
a much

The cardinal, in obedience to the emperor's commands, put off his journey towards *England* till some more convenient time. In the mean while the queen's marriage with the prince of *Spain* was

---

a much fairer diadem, *the crown of England*, in recompence for his loss. An enthusiastic PORTUGUESE once prophesied this good fortune to him (Quirini, vol. iii. ep. 19.) and his bigoted admirers afterwards aided the deceit; yet there seems to be no solid foundation in the truth of history for so chimerical a dream—MARY's pride and passions more strongly inclined her to a *younger king* than to an *older cardinal*; nay, could she have stooped to a subject, COURTENAY seemed to have fairer pretensions to her favour than POLE, as the French embassador NOAILLES (a very shrewd observer) often took notice of— GRATIANI indeed (in his life of COMMENDONE) asserts, that the queen asked *him*, "if the pope could grant a dispensation "for a cardinal deacon to marry?" but VERTOT, who relates this story from GRATIANI, gives no credit to it, because M. DE NOAILLES makes no mention of it in his dispatches to his court, but only as the idle apprehension of GARDINER.

T. PHILIPS indeed boldly delivers this report of GRATIANI's (very dubious as it is) for an historical truth; but the real cause why CHARLES V. detained POLE on the continent, was, not his jealousy of him, as a rival to his son, but as too eager a promoter of the religious changes; it was to prevent the affairs of religion (which were far from being the first object either with the queen or himself) from interfering with the SPANISH MATCH.

Le parlement doit finir demain (says M. NOAILLES to the king of *France*, in his letter of May 4, 1554) *sans aucune reformation de la religion, que cette princesse a bien voulu remettre en autre temps, pour avancer & feliciter ce qu' elle a plus en affection.*—

resolved

resolved on in the *English* council; whereupon Pole sent Peter Soto (who had been the emperor's confessor, and was at that time at *Dilinghen*, where he had a seminary of young students under his tuition) to sollicit his Imperial majesty's permission to proceed on his journey.

The emperor readily consented, and Pole immediately set forward and came to *Brussels* [g], where his majesty then kept his court, who received him with great courtesy; but as the match was not abso-

---

[g] The cardinal, after many rebuffs from the emperor, who treated him as the meanest tool of his power, was at last, upon his humble supplication, suffered to advance as far as *Brussels*, where he was so far from meeting with the *courtesy* which Beccatelli mentions, that Charles treated him with his usual contempt.

" Ce prince lui dit *avec dureté*, qu'il se seroit bien dispensé
" de la peine qu'il avoit prise de revenir."
Noailles, vol. iii. p. 187, note.

Here he was kept " envelopé sous les ailes de cette grande
" aigle," till he should choose to let him loose for some convenient services; and when the cardinal, not so unmindful of his personal interests as his biographers would suppose him, had applied from thence to the queen, to be restored to his family estate—Charles gave him to understand,

Si le dit *cardinal* vouloit maintenant avoir quelque bien en *Angleterre*, ou autrement demander quelque chose, *il faudroit parler au lui meme*.
Noailles, Avis au Roi, 13 Mai, 1554.

lutely settled, nor the prince of *Spain* yet arrived in *England*, the emperor, for the reasons before suggested, to guard against every possible ill consequence, signified his pleasure that the cardinal should defer his voyage a little longer, till news came of his son's landing, which was expected every day. Pole was all compliance [a], and in the *interim*, as hostilities still continued between the *French* and *Flemings*, being impowered by the

---

[a] During his stay at *Brussels* he drew up that *vehement remonstrance* against the *form* of the *Act of parliament*, *passed in the first sessions of queen Mary's reign, to confirm the legitimacy of her mother's marriage*, on account of the omission of *the papal dispensation*. Here his furious zeal for the *power of the keys* has made him so far o'erleap all bounds, that in endeavouring to prove the necessity of the pope's dispensation to validate that match, he has most evidently shewn it was absolutely *indispensable*.

" The marriage itself (says he) was not only *tacitly*, but
" *expresly* contradictory to the law of the Old Testament, that
" a brother should not marry a brother's wife, but also of the
" *New*, confirmed moreover by a general council, received
" by the whole church, and enrolled among the statute-laws
" of *England*. In this case therefore the queen had no other
" resource but the INEXPUGNABILE PROPUGNACULUM AU-
" THORITATIS PONTIFICIÆ."
Scriptum tertium C. Poli, Quirini, vol. v. p. 171.

Surely if *that match* was so notoriously repugnant to so many irrefragable obligations, every *divine* revelation, and every HUMAN institution; this INEXPUGNABILE PROPUGNACULUM, as he weakly calls it, could not support its validity!

pope

pope for that purpose, he began to treat with the emperor upon the most feasible method to put an end, if possible, to so long and calamitous a war. The pope had, a few months before, dispatched two legates from *Rome* on the same commission; Cardinal DANDINO to the *Imperial* court, and the Cardinal of ST. GEORGE to the *French*; but their embassies had proved fruitless: Nevertheless the emperor listened favourably to POLE, and told him, he should sift the king of *France*'s inclinations on that point; that for his part he was ready to accept of honourable terms of accommodation. On these overtures the cardinal set forward for PARIS, where he had a long audience of the king, in which he expatiated with the freedom becoming a legate of the holy see, both in presence of the KING and the *Constable of France*, upon the unhappy discord which had so long subsisted between the two crowns. HENRY II. was so pleased with his *Eminence*, that he expressed publickly, " how [1] sorry he was, not to have known the car-
" dinal's

---

[1] In consequence of this courtly compliment from HENRY II. of *France*, POLE applied to that monarch the year following for his interest in the conclave on the death of Julius III. March 23, 1554—The confident he made use of was his old trusty servant the Abbé DI SAN SALUTE, who promised NOAILLES, " that if his master would do his utmost to raise POLE to the popedom, he would not go to Rome till he had finished the business then in hand; that then he would pass through *France*, to testify his obligation to the king, and convince

"dinal's merits on the death of PAUL III. which, if he had done, no one should have had his interest for the popedom but POLE; that he greatly regretted he was so ill informed at that time;" and then dismissed him with full hopes of an accommodation. But the wounds were, alas! too much exulcerated to be soon healed.

---

vince him of his future resolutions to be grateful to him for that service.

Noailles, vol. iv. p. 382.

T. PHILIPS takes no notice of this *second* canvass for the papal chair, and the private manner in which it was done thro' the Abbé PARPALIA.

On the death of MARCELLUS II, (May 1, 1555) the constable of *Montmorenci* makes POLE the same compliments his master had made him before, apologizes for his former disappointments, and offers him a fresh tender of HENRY's services; though CARAFFA's success seemed to please that court much better, as the cardinal's attachment to the imperial faction was well known to that king and his ministers.

The queen also (as T. PHILIPS tells us from BENNET) endeavoured to recommend her favourite on the death of MARCELLUS II. and it is pleasant to see how busy GARDINER shewed himself in haranguing upon the merits of a man he disliked, and whose abilities he had no high opinion of, that he might get him out of his way, and secure the legateship, on POLE's promotion, to himself.

Il me fut aisé à croire (says Noailles) que le chancelier voudroit fort le promotion du dit C. POLUS, pour l'assurance qu'il auroit d avoir sa legation.

Noailles au connetable, 15 May 1555.

In the mean while Philip, prince of *Spain*, to the great joy of the queen and the emperor, arrived in *England* in the month of July; soon after which the marriage was solemnized with great pomp and festivity.

The [k] cardinal's presence in *England* was at this time very much in request, and would have been very seasonable to complete the re-establishment of

---

[k] Either the cardinal's long absence from his country, or his extravagant zeal for the *Romish* faith, had extinguished every spark of *patriotism* in his bosom, or one sigh must have escaped him upon the melancholy prospect of its becoming soon a province of Spain, through this fatal marriage of the Queen of England; but instead of that, he is rapturous even to a degree of profaneness in his encomiums upon the match, which, he says, in a letter to pope Julius III. dated Nov. 30, 1554.

"Resembled the marriage of that great king, who, though
"heir of the whole world, was sent down by his father from
"his royal mansions, to become the spouse and son of a Vir-
"gin, and the Comforter and Saviour of the whole race of man-
"kind; for so did this greatest of all kings, the heir of his
"father, leave his large and opulent dominions for the sake of
"this factious kingdom, and become the *spouse* and *son* of a virgin
"(for though he be her spouse, he behaves to her as though he
"were her son) that he might be the mediator and intercessor
"to reconcile this nation to Christ and his church."

Quirini, vol. v. epist. 1.

Let Thomas Philips declare, whether the man who could write such a letter as this, be not *a profane flatterer, an enemy to the true interest of his country*, and *an enthusiastic madman*.

the

the church upon its former foundation. But either envy, ambition, or some other restless spirit, instigated a party there to labour secretly to undermine him, and erect their own fortunes upon his ruin. With this view many ill-offices [1] were done to him at the Imperial court, at *Rome*, and in *England*. Upon which his *Eminence* used to compare himself to a person wrestling in a meadow of unmowed grass, who sees the surface waving by the motion of a snake underneath, tho' he cannot exactly distinguish the spot where he lurks. In these distresses his recourse was to God in prayer, imploring him to give his blessing to a cause peculiarly his own; and if he himself was too weak

---

[1] The busy importunity of the court of *Rome* to interfere in the new model of the *English* government, which was now to take place on MARY's accession, was displeasing to all parties; the emperor was the first to resent it, and he did it, we find, with the *orgullo* of a *Spaniard*. The chancellor GARDINER was very peevish on POLE's busying himself daily, by letters or messengers, in all their public proceedings; nay, the queen herself, who was afraid of losing her husband through the injudicious importunity of her legate, could scarcely keep her temper with him, while he was constantly teazing her from MAGUZANO, DILINGHEM, or BRUSSELS, with advices and remonstrances, which she was resolved not to regard till she had carried a more favourite point, *her match with the prince of Spain*, which, had not the 1,200,000 crowns sent by the emperor reconciled to the *English* parliament, the queen had probably been forced to have kept the promises made with the *Suffolk men*, and the cardinal never had set his foot again in ENGLAND.

an

CARDINAL REGINALD POLE.   95

an inſtrument to promote it, he begged to be removed from it. But truth at length triumphed over malice, and blazed forth with a luſtre not to be concealed.

MARY came to a reſolution of recalling the cardinal to England in ſpite of all oppoſition, and an act of parliament was immediately paſſed to repeal all ſtatutes of treaſon and attainder made by Henry VIII. againſt POLE and his family, and to reſtore him in blood with particular marks of diſtinction. To bring him home to his country with extraordinary honours, ſhe ſent two of the principal perſons of her court, Lord PAGET, and Lord EDWARD HASTINGS, her maſter of the horſe, with a ſumptuous retinue to wait for him at *Bruſſels*. Thus attended he took his leave of the emperor, and embarked at *Calais* for *England*, in November 1554 [m], and was received on his coming aſhore by two

---

[m] The *Curators* of the *Quirinian* library at *Breſcia*, who publiſhed the Vth *volume of cardinal Pole's Letters*, &c. after the deceaſe of the firſt projector of that work, C. Quirini (who lived to publiſh only four volumes, but left ſufficient materials among the MSS. in his library for the completion of a fifth volume) have been very diligent in collecting together, for the ſubſtance of the concluding volume, whatever the archives of their maſter's library could furniſh them with, any-ways relative to the life or writings of *his* and *their* favourite *idol*, REGINALD POLE —Among others, they have given us, in their appendix, a curious *Italian letter* written from *London* to a friend at *Rome* (probably by Binardi, or Floribello, or Fr. Stella, or ſome other Italian

two reprefentatives of the whole nobility, a fpiritual and a temporal lord, who came by exprefs orders from the queen and the two ftates, to prefent him the bill which had lately paffed the houfes for reftoring the honours of his family, which, as a peculiar mark of diftinction, was fealed with *a golden feal* [n]. He was accompanied the whole way,

---

Italian, in the cardinal's retinue) on the 1ft of Decem. 1554, which gives a very pompous and poffibly an exact detail of the legate's magnificent proceffion, public entry, and the whole ceremony of reconciling the nation to the Romifh church; beginning from his departure from *Bruffels*, Nov. 13, and ending with the account of the lord mayor's vifit to him at *Lambeth* on Saturday Dec. 1, requefting him to make his folemn proceffion through the city on the morrow to hear a fermon at St. Paul's from the lord chancellor and bifhop of Winchefter, GARDINER.

This letter, or tract, is intituled, " Il feliciffimo Ritorno del " Regno d'Inghilterra all' obedienza della Sede Apoftolica," Quirini, vol. v. p. 303.

DUDITHIUS feems to have been indebted to this work for many particulars in his account of POLE's return to *England*, which are not to be found in BECCATELLI; and PHILIPS has made frequent ufe of it, though not with the greateft judgment.

[n] This particular mark of diftinction affixed to POLE's pardon, was in return to a compliment a former pope, CLEMENT VII. had paid to HENRY VIII. (and which that popifh parliament adopted to do honour to the legate) who, when he confirmed to him the title of FIDEI DEFENSOR conferred on him by LEO X. fent him *a bull with a golden feal appendant to it*; which is engraved by Rymer, tom. xiv. p. 14.

from

Cardinal REGINALD POLE.

from his first landing till he came to *London*, by numerous attendance of prelates and peers, to do him honour both as a nobleman and a legate of the holy see, now come °to bring a blessing upon his country after an absence of 20 years; and upon his arrival in *London* he was ushered, with every testimony of exultation, into the royal palace. As he sailed up the *Thames*, with a vast train of barges to escort him, the king came down to the water-side to do him honour; and when one of the lords, who thought the condescension too great, observed, " Your majesty is going *to wait* on your *subject*,".

° The archdeacon of *Canterbury*, where POLE lay the first night, upon his road from *Dover*, complimented him in a Latin oration, of which *the Italian writer of the Ritorno*, &c. has quoted a particular passage, which has a conceit in it that seemed to strike his ear; which T. PHILIPS will please to allow to be as true a specimen of the taste of that reign, as the *Jeu de mots* in the *Oxford* declamation to Queen *Elizabeth*, which he is so incensed at, was of the succeeding.
Life of Pole, vol. ii. p. 117.

Tu es POLUS! qui aperis nobis POLUM cœlorum.
Ritorno, &c. vol. v. p. 307. Quirini.

And this *Wit of Canterbury* is still more inexcusable than the *Oxford Punster*, for he repeats the same *pun* in his funeral oration on the cardinal, which he had before broached on his first welcome to *Canterbury*.

—O salutarem illum diem, quo POLUS noster non dubito quin a cœlesti illo *Polo* missus nos Deo & ecclesiæ reddidit—
Funebris Oratio, Quirini, vol. v. p. 192.

the

the king replied, "I go to pay due honour to *the Legate of the Holy See.*" The queen * waited for him on the stairs, and both their majesties caressed him in the most courteous manner.

THE queen had given orders for the archbishop's palace in *London*, situated opposite to the royal palace, to be furnished for his reception; which he found fitted up according to the *English* fashion with great magnificence, and also a sumptuous train of officers and attendants, not to be supported but by a princely revenue.

As it had been resolved in the house some days before, to perform a solemn act of reconciliation to the church of *Rome*, orders were given to set apart St. *Andrew's* day for that service; when the House should meet in the *Great Chamber* of the palace, and

---

P A most extraordinary speech made by the cardinal legate to the queen (upon the king's making him take her majesty's right-hand as they walked, and placing himself on her left) may be worth recording, to shew, that when a CARDINAL makes a compliment, though to a queen, it centers in a greater one to his own person:

"V. Maestà ha da ringratiar grandemente, perche la giunta
" infieme le due maggior potestà del mondo; cioe quella della
" Maestà della imperatore rappresentata nella Maestà del Rè,
" & quella della Santità del Papa, rappresentata *nella persona
" mia.*"

Il Felic. Ritorno.

the

the legate should be present and give them his benediction.

The king and queen, and the two q states of parliament, assembled on the day appointed, and the legate was introduced with full pomp, attended with all the ensigns of his high character, when he made r an elegant speech in his own native tongue, and was seconded by the bishop of WINCHESTER, lord chancellor, who dwelt much on the extraordinary mercies of God to this kingdom, " which had pre-" served s this *angelic minister* for their sakes, who came

---

q It is to be lamented that the ignominious acts of this day were not for ever expunged out of the annals of our history— One may forgive the vanity of a *foreigner* and an *Italian*, if he exults in the triumphs of his master, at whose side perhaps he stood, and beheld the two states of our infatuated country lying prostrate at the feet of a popish legate ; but, had he lived to mark the glorious annals of the succeeding reign, he would have acknowleged " *England triumphed in her turn, and made* " *ample atonement for one inglorious* lustrum *of bigotry and sla-* " *very, by the prosperous establishment of true religion and national* " *honour, under a long and successful period of five-and-forty* " *years.*"

r The speech which POLE spoke in *English* before the house, was translated afterwards into *Latin* at his own request by ROGER ASCHAM, that it might be transmitted to the pope.

s This *hypocritical rant* of GARDINER's in praise of a man he was known to dislike, whose *angelic mission* he had long struggled to render abortive, by keeping him by every possible artifice

"came to lead them out of darkness into light, thro' this their present act of obedience to the apostolic see, which their ancestors had always acknowledged."

THE whole assembly unanimously declared, they would never swerve from their obedience, and asking pardon *three* several times for their former transgressions, begged his reconciling benediction; which the legate pronounced before them all, the king and queen standing, and the whole house upon their knees, weeping tears of joy for so marvellous a blessing [t]. This done, they broke up full of

---

fice out of the kingdom; and whose cause (that of restoring the *papal supremacy* over this nation) he had publickly *written against*, must, one would have imagined, have disturbed the mock solemnity of that day, and have thrown the whole house into a burst of laughter, had not *Spanish gravity* infected the whole assembly, or *Spanish gold* reconciled barefaced knavery as well as bigotry to their deluded senses.

[t] Our English annalists and historians, STRYPE, FOX, HEYLIN, and others, to make the contrast between MARY's reign and her successor's appear more striking, say but little to palliate this dastardly humiliation of a *British* house of parliament, but agree in painting them all like so many wretched *mendicants* under the lash of their *penitentiary*. But the *French* embassador, who was present, saw the inward discontent that sat brooding over the hearts of many among them— "*L'occa-*
"*sion de sa venue ameyne quelque regret à plusieurs,*" and he imputes their *apparent* satisfaction to the great cunning and subtlety of
Gardiner's

of gratitude and thankſgiving, and went in a body to the chapel-royal to ſing *Te Deum*.

The next object of the queen's attention was the re-eſtabliſhment of the *monks*, who were called back into *England*, while the *hereticks*, who had crouded

---

Gardiner's miniſtry, and the dextrous application of the imperial dollars.

" Tant les ſujets de ce royaume ſont maniez dextrement &
" de grand artifice."
Negociations de Noailles, vol. iv. p. 25.

Monſ. l'Abbé Vertot (in his *Introduction* to theſe letters of Noailles, from the ſubſtance of which he has compiled a ſhort hiſtory of that period) deſcribes the manner in which the two houſes ſubmitted themſelves to the *papal yoke*, with a ſpirit leſs unbecoming the name of *Engliſhmen*.

" Il (Polus) donna abſolution generale, ſans oſer exiger ni
" penitence ni reſtitution ; il fallut pardonner ſans conditions
" des fautes qu'il eût été dangereux de vouloir punir; on ſe
" contenta des *fieres ſatisfactions des Anglois, dont la plupart*
" *reçurent cette grace, comme s'ils l'avoient faites eux-mêmes au*
" *Souverain Pontife.*"
Vertot Introduct. aux Lettres de Noailles, vol. i. p. 302.

Father Paul's account of Pole's reception ſeems alſo more worthy the genius of this nation, equally repugnant to *civil and religious ſlavery*.

Fu aggradita la perſona del Cardinale (Polo) & alla propoſitione fu preſtato *apparente* aſſenſo, ſe bene nel ſecreto la maggior parte *abborriva la qualità di Miniſtro Pontificio*, & ſentiva diſpiacere di ritornar ſotto il giogo.
Iſtoria del Con. di Trento, lib. 4to.

in from all quarters, were driven out in their turn; also *catholic* bishops were promoted to the vacant sees, and *heretical* [u] ones removed to make way for them. How worthy they were of their preferments their behaviour shewed afterwards, when, upon the changes which took place in the nation upon the death of queen MARY, they chose rather to be degraded, and forfeit their revenues, and be thrown into prisons, with the farther hazard of their lives, than give up their allegiance to the church of *Rome*. Among other vacancies, the archbishoprick of *Canterbury*, the metropolitan see of ENGLAND, was one, which the queen [w], in whom

the

---

[u] BECCATELLI, who wrote to please the ears of the friends to the papacy, is very free in his language, and paints the queen's zeal in its true colours, who exerted herself very early *discacciando gli heretici*—I must beg leave to apologize to my protestant readers for my *literal* translation of my author's expressions, in the words of *the learned translator of Du Pin's Ecclesiastical History*—

"It was debated whether the words *heretic, schismatic,* &c. should not be left out; that *reformation* should be substituted for *heresy*, and *popish* for *catholic*; but upon mature deliberation it was resolved the author's words should be strictly kept to; since, in a history, we desire not only matter of fact, but the relator's own way of telling it, to be kept intire"—

Du Pin's Ecclesiastical History, 16th century.

[w] The sword, which king PHILIP drew on his landing at *Southampton*, was the signal of vengeance and persecution against

the

the nomination was, determined in favour of the cardinal, as she thought it fitting the first dignity in the church should be conferred on the churchman of the first rank and quality in her kingdom, who would have great influence over the other prelates both by his example and authority.

---

the name of PROTESTANTISM, which was devoted to the slaughter, as a victim to those unhallowed nuptials, and only respited for a short season, till ROME should send over her own *high-priest* to offer up the devoted *holocaust*.

Although T. PHILIPS may affect to smile at these horrid tales, as if invented only to throw infamy on that detested reign, yet, however he may choose to discredit the accounts of *Protestant* historians, he will certainly admit the testimony of a professed *Jesuit* on this point:

Father ORLEANS will tell him what followed immediately after the queen's marriage, and the nation's reconciliation with the church of *Rome*.

" Ce fut ensuite de cette *reunion* qu'on commença à exercer
" contre les protestans la rigueur dont toutes les histoires se
" plaignent ; on en fit en effet mourir un grand nombre."

Le caractere d'esprit de MARIE lui inspiroit naturellement cet excés de severité ; elle en usa envers la pluspart de ceux qui lui avoient eté contraires—S'etant ainsi defaites de ses plus dangereux ennemis, elle fut bientot en etat d'exercer la même rigueur sur ceux de l'église, s'ils s'obstinoient à la combattre—Ce fut un des motifs qui lui fit prendre la resolution d'epouser PHILIPPE II. alors prince d'Espagne.

Pere d'Orleans, Revolutions d'Angleterre, 1554.

POPE JULIUS [x] made great rejoicings at *Rome* on the news of the late reconciliation of the *English* church and nation, and proclaimed a *jubilee extraordinary* on that account.

THE queen also, in the name of herself and her kingdom, sent three ambassadors, representing the three states of the nation, to do their homage to

---

[x] An *Italian* letter from *Rome*, in answer to the *Felicissimo Ritorno* &c. mentioned before, describes the extraordinary festivities kept by the pope and his cardinals, on the first news of this great revolution in *England*; one can scarce speak of the superstitious ceremonies observed on that occasion, and be serious.

JULIUS III. in honour of the patron saint of *that* day, heard mass in the chapel of *St. Andrea*, " nell giorno della " cui festa seguiva cosi santo & meraviglioso effetto." I am not " sufficiently versed in the *Romish legends* to know when and by whom this good apostle's *head* was brought from *Constantinople*, where it had been deposited in the great chapel by CONSTANTINE, but we now find it at *Rome*, and we are told in the same Italian letter,

" *La Testa* di *S. Andrea* tutta il giorno fu scoperta, accioché dà tutti potesse esser veduta, visitata, & *riverita*,
Appendix, vol. v. Quirini, p. 323.

Lord HERBERT tells a story, " that *a finger* of this saint " had been pawned by a needy convent for 50 l. which was " left unredeemed by the poor friers at the dissolution of it;" may we not suppose, that the broker now disposed of it to the cardinal, or some of his zealous houshold, for at least ten times its original pledge?

CARDINAL REGINALD POLE.   103

the pope; the bishop of ELY on the part of the clergy, the Lord MONTAGUE for the lords, and Sir EDWARD CARNE, an eminent civilian (who resided there afterwards in quality of ambassador [y]) in behalf of the commons of the realm. This embassy was scarcely arrived in *Italy*, when news met them of the death of the pope, which happened in March 1555, in whose stead succeeded MARCELLUS, lately known by the name of the Cardinal DI SANTA CROCE, who gave orders for the reception and entertainment of the *English* ambassadors at *Bologna* at the public expence. This pope died within 20 days; the news of whose death (as [z] I was informed by some who

were

---

[y] Sir EDWARD CARNE was the last embassador from *England* to the court of *Rome*, till JAMES II. sent Lord CASTLEMAIN in 1686, one of whose important errands was,

"To procure a dispensation for Father PETRE the *Jesuit* to enjoy an *English* bishoprick."

Rapin's Hist. James II.

[z] I do not find any reason for supposing BECCATELLI to have attended POLE into *England* (as QUIRINI asserts) but rather the contrary, and for these reasons—He never mentions it himself; his translator DUDITHIUS who mentions FLOREBELLO, STELLA, and others, takes no notice of it; his account of POLE's public entry does not seem so circumstantial as one would have expected from an eye-witness, neither does he seem to have known the situation of *Lambeth-palace*, when he says of it, "*posto in* LONDRA *dirimpetto a quello del Rè.*" The

present

were present) so afflicted C. POLE, that he wept much when he heard it, and said to his attendants, "I grieve for the impending calamities of the church, which I now plainly foresee will be the consequence of the loss of this excellent pontiff." The cardinal of *Naples*, called afterwards * Paul IV. succeeded

---

present passage confirms me still in this opinion, as he was certainly not in *England* at MARCELLUS's death, which was not above *six months* after POLE's arrival in *England*, and therefore probably never came here at all.

* Neither BECCATELLI nor DUDITHIUS mention POLE's being a candidate for the popedom, upon either of the two last vacancies on the deaths of JULIUS or MARCELLUS. But T. PHILIPS (upon the strength of a mere letter of compliment from the constable MONTMORENCI to POLE, which he found in the Ambassade de Noailles, and MARY's instruction to GARDINER to apply for him in her name) with his usual parade pronounces (vol. ii. p. 105.)

"That *two* rival crowns, who had opposite views in all "other concerns, seemed to vie with each other, and to have "but one common interest when the commendation of C. POLE "was the theme, or his advancement the prize."—

How smoothly words flow along, when unembarrassed with reason or argument!

The *Lettres de Noailles* shew, that POLE *applied* to the court of *France* for that king's interest on the death of JULIUS by the Abbé di S. SALUTE (17 Avril 1555)—but MARCELLUS succeeded; the French cardinals did nothing for POLE; and the constable tells him by NOAILLES, "He must acquiesce in an "event which God had ordained" (21 Avril 1555)—MAR-

CELLUS

succeeded him in the chair, March 22d, and received the homage of the *English* ambassadors in full *consistory*, where an elegant oration was spoken by the bishop of ELY.

DURING this interval the queen of ENGLAND, at the instance of Cardinal POLE, endeavoured to mediate a peace between the emperor and the king of *France*, who, in compliment to her majesty, agreed to send their ministers to a *congress* to be holden at *Ardres* near *Calais*, a place within the queen of *England*'s territories in PICARDY. Upon this occasion a magnificent pavilion was erected at the queen's expence, formed with distinct apartments for the reception of the several plenipotentiaries, her majesty dispatched thither some of the principal lords of her court, with Cardinal POLE at their

---

CELLUS dies.——The constable renews his promise to POLE——and orders Noailles to give him the fullest assurances " pour tenir " en meilleur disposition (10 May 1555)—— GARDINER also applies in the legate's favour, but with the view only of succeeding him (as NOAILLES observes, 15 Mai 1555) in his legateship——The election comes on——Caraffa succeeds——and NOAILLES remarks upon it, " That *he* would be a fa-" vourer of his master's interest ;" which he certainly never could hope of POLE, and was therefore undoubtedly better pleased that the other succeeded to the popedom.

What becomes now of " *The two rival crowns vying with* " *each other in commendation of Pole ?*"

head.

head. But every trouble and expence [b] proved fruitless at this conference, altho' the cardinal did all possible good offices, both with the *Imperial* and *French* ministers, in order to effect an accommodation.

THE queen now sent to *Rome* a list of the persons which she named to the vacant sees, which, when MORONE proceeded according to custom, to *propose* in the consistory, by virtue of his office of *Cardinal Protector of England*, the pope stopped him, telling him to leave what respected the archbishop of *Canterbury* [c] to himself. This ceremony he

---

[b] This pompous and expensive conference at *La Marque* (which T. PHILIPS has given a fuller detail of from the Ambassade de NOAILLES) was attended with the usual ill success which marked POLE's negotiations; it was brought on by MARY, to keep her husband at home, who was in a great hurry to leave her, and in effect did so within three months after the congress broke up, when the queen grew sick of so great an expence which had not answered its purpose, and levied a tax upon the city of LONDON for the payment of it.

" L'on a mis une taille en cette ville pour payer les frais
" qui ont eté faits en cet abouchement par ceux-ci; dont les
" habitans se plaignent beaucoup, & disent; qu'ils en tireront
" trois fois plus qu'ils ont couté; qu'est une chose qui fait
" bien paroitre la necessité d'argent qu'ils ont." (Negociat. de Noailles, 14 Jun. 1555.)

[c] Both BECCATELLI and PRIULI seem to have shewn great tenderness for their patron's honour, in observing so scrupulous a silence

he afterwards executed himself in person, with signal expressions of honour both towards the queen and the cardinal, bearing testimony to POLE's great learning and eminent endowments, and enlarging much on his many distinguished virtues, which, he said, he had been acquainted with for many years past.

THE form of *Provision* to the see of CANTERBURY [d] being returned to ENGLAND, and the cardinal ordained

---

a silence with regard to his suffering predecessor, CRANMER, whose name they do not so much as mention, when they speak of the cardinal's promotion to the see of *Canterbury*, neither BECCATELLI in his history, nor PRIULI in his Italian letter to his friend BECCATELLI at *Ragusa*, written from *London* in 1556, wherein he informs him of several other bloody acts of religious persecution, which were transacting about the same period. Their deliberate silence on so *eminent a sufferer* (in whose fall they would have certainly exulted with all the triumphant malice of a COLE or a PHILIPS, could they have done it to the honour of their master) is to me a tacit reproach on POLE's memory for the cruel part he acted in that *mockery of religious justice,*—THE BRINGING THAT GOOD MAN TO THE STAKE.

[d] I would wish that every person (who is not disposed to give T. PHILIPS implicit credit for the bold panegyric he has passed upon POLE's remarkable letter to *Cranmer*) would be at the pains to read it over, tedious as it may be, in the works of LE GRAND or QUIRINI. They may then judge whether it be, as he defines it (vol. ii. p. 147.) "One of the most complete pieces of controversy that ever was penn'd."

But

dained *prieſt*, he ſung his firſt maſs in the church of *St. Mary le Bow*, the principal pariſh under the archiepiſcopal juriſdiction in LONDON, where he was attended by a great concourſe of the nobility and clergy: after which he preached a ſermon in his native tongue, as he did frequently afterwards in many churches of his dioceſs, and alſo at *Canter-*

But were it all this and more (which it is as widely diſtant from, as the late HISTORY OF THE LIFE OF CARDINAL POLE is from truth and candour) yet ſuch a letter written to an unhappy man, under the miſeries of a priſon, muſt be an indelible reproach to the memory of the writer.—One extract will be ſufficient to unfold the genius and temper of the whole.

He tells CRANMER, "He comes now to talk *mildly* with
" him in the name of the church; if he ſpake in his own
" name, he ſhould rather call on God to caſt down fire from
" heaven on him, and the priſon where he lay, for forſaking
" the church."

After this *mild* preamble, he thus enters on his invectives, Vous avez imité le ſerpent &c.

" You have followed the example of the infernal ſerpent;
" you have practiſed all your wiles to deſtroy the king and
" kingdom, and the whole church; to plunge into utter ruin
" ſo many thouſand men; for are you not guilty of all the
" calamities that have fallen upon this nation?"—

The poor priſoner would have but little inclination to go through a letter which treated him with ſuch indecent malignity in the very firſt page; neither do I think it poſſible for a man of common humanity to take it up now (tho' 200 years afterwards) without throwing it aſide with indignation and abhorrence.

bury,

bury, where he would fain have fixed his abode, and kept that constant residence which became a good pastor; but the queen would never suffer him to leave the court, insisting, that it was more for the interest of the catholic faith that he should reside near her person, than at *Canterbury*, which was also at no incompetent distance from the metropolis. Many able divines were consulted on this point, who assured the cardinal, that he could not, with a safe conscience, abandon her majesty, *when [e] there was so much business to be done, to crush the heretics, and give new life to the catholic cause.*

---

[e] BECCATELLI has very strongly express'd the true purport of the queen and her ministry, in the Italian;

"Tanto bisogno che si trovava, per opprimere li heretici, & aiutare i cattolici."

These few words seem to comprehend the whole passion and ambition of the queen, and in effect the whole business of her reign.

The French ambassador then resident at *London*, who may be presumed to have had no partial affection for the nation, speaks with horror at the cruelties that daily passed before his eyes.

"Les plus beaux spectacles que l'on puisse voir en cette ville, & par tout ce pays, ce sont gibets accomgnez des plus braves & vaillants hommes, qu'elle eut point en son royaume, etant par tout les prisons si pleines de cette noblesse, & autres plus apparens de ce peuple, qu'il est force que les uns par leur mort cedent la place aux autres, qui journellement y sont amenez de toutes parts."

(Mr. Noailles a Mr. D'Oysel, vol. iii. 21 Fev. 1553.

THE

THE next object of the queen's attention was to restore the ecclesiastical ᶠ revenues, which HENRY VIII. had sequestered; to effectuate which her majesty was content to relinquish whatever had been vested in the crown, which amounted to the full moiety of the ancient patrimony of the church; as for the remainder, which had been dissipated among private proprietors, it was suffered to continue to the several possessors, by the connivance of the pope, to avoid giving uneasiness to the subjects in the infancy of these changes, not doubting but in course of time they would restore all the churches and the ᵍ revenues which belonged to them.

IN

ᶠ This act of the queen's was strongly opposed by many judicious members of the legislature at the first, for *two* very sensible reasons; 1st. The great impoverishing of the civil list, of which foreign courts would take advantage (of which Noailles immediately gave notice to his master, Negoc. vol. iv.) 2dly, The insidious view the queen had in it, to make a future pretence of it for obliging her lay-subjects to do the same.

Most probably (says a catholic writer much quoted by T. PHILIPS) if the queen had lived a few years longer, either love to her, or *fear of the king's displeasure*, or *dread of incurring the pope's curse*, and the church's censures, would have influenced many to restore the church lands. (HISTORICAL COLLECTIONS).

ᵍ This being a subject of too interesting a nature, for a clergyman to expect that much weight will be allowed to his own opinions upon it, I shall leave it open, after giving POLE's immediate successor's sentiments on the little advantage that accrued

CARDINAL REGINALD POLE. 111

In the year 1556 the queen of *England*, in conjunction with the *French* ministers, wrought so effectually as to bring about a truce [b], or suspension of hostilities, for five years betwen the emperor and the king of FRANCE, which gave great hopes of peace to all Christendom.

---

crued to the CHURCH, by what MARY relinquished, or her ARCHBISHOP disposed of, for the supposed benefit of the clergy.

ARCHBISHOP PARKER says, (Antiq. Eccles. Brit. fol. p. 528.)

"This reliction of the first-fruits and tenths by MARY was more prejudicial than beneficial to the clergy, who still continued to pay them (by POLE's order, to whom that affair was intrusted) after the queen had given them up, under pretence of support for the monks and religious, whom HENRY VIII. had turned out, lest the royal revenue should be burdened beyond what it could bear by this liberality of the queen's.—POLE deducted but a small portion of that money for the support of the *mendicants*, and reserved the residue to himself, which brought him great wealth which he left wholly to foreigners."

[b] *The treaty of Vaucelles* between CHARLES V. and HENRY II. was concluded on the part of those two crowns by COLIGNI and LELAIN, without the mediation, or least concurrence of the queen of *England* or her legate, to the great chagrin of them both (as M. NOAILLES tells MONTMORENCI, 12 Mars 1555) "Si est ce qu'ils ne peuvent tant dissimuler leur passion, que l'on ne connoisse evidement, qu'ils n'ont pas grand contentement que ce marchè se soit fait sans y mouiller les doits."

(Negoc. de Noailles, vol. v. p. 312.)

BUT

But *Satan*, who is ever conspiring against the interest and happiness of mankind, put it in the head of pope PAUL IV. to expel King PHILIP out of the kingdom of *Naples*, for which purpose he sent his nephew Cardinal CARAFFA in quality of legate to the court of *France*, to prevail upon HENRY II. to engage [1] in an alliance with him against PHILIP, and either thro' jealousy of POLE's too great influence over the queen of *England*, who had been in-

---

[1] The rupture betweed PAUL IV. and PHILIP (in which POLE busied himself too officiously, probably by the commands of his mistress, who hazarded every thing to gratify her husband) which BECCATELLI here ascribes to the instigations of SATAN, and T. PHILIPS reproaches the pope for in the bitterest language, appears from the testimony of Cardinal MORONE, who had no great occasion to speak partially of PAUL IV. to have taken its rise on the pope's part from very urgent and repeated provocations. In a letter to POLE from ROME (June 1556) he repeats many insults offered to the papal authority both in NAPLES and SICILY, the dominions of PHILIP, and then gives his own sentiments upon the matter with great candour.

" Io ingenuamente confesso a V. S. illustrissima, che mi par, " che suà santità ha molta ragione intorno a queste materie," Quirini, vol. v. let. 50. and in the 51st letter he writes again on the same subject, viz.

La defensione è *de jure naturæ*, nostro signore attenderè a defendersi, ma li adversarii, pare, che minacciano di volerci far danno. Io prego ancora V. S. voglia advertir quel sereniffimo rè, che le cause di far guerra contra sede apostolica, perche il papa habbia privato un suo suddito non e giusta.

strumental

strumental in making the late truce between those two crowns, or from a former pique he had taken against him, or from some late misreports of POLE's enemies, he recalled the legate, and appointed GUL. PETO ZOCCOLANTE [k], whom he made cardinal for that purpose, to be his legate at the court of *England* in his stead. PETO was a steady catholic, and a man of character, and had been well known to POLE during the time he spent in *Italy*; but being much advanced in years, and of ignoble birth, the queen did not think him qualified for that high office in her kingdom, and being much displeased with this appointment [l] of the pope's,

---

[k] *This zealous and religious personage* (as T. PHILIPS characterises him) *William Peto, the Franciscan*, to whom BECCATELLI, in honour of his being made a cardinal, has affixed the additional name *Zoccolante*, tho' of *ignoble birth*, and as *ignobly* spoken of by our annalist *Stow*, by the title of "One friar *Peto*, a simple man, yet very devout, of the order of the Observants," had yet very early merits with the court of Rome, and of the same kind with those which first recommended his brother-legate, POLE, viz. "a most insolent and personal abuse of his sovereign, Henry VIII." for which he is loudly celebrated by the AUTHOR of the HISTORICAL COLLECTIONS, from whence it is transcribed by T. PHILIPS (vol. i. p. 187, note.)

[l] In this act of revoking C. POLE's legatine powers, and recalling him to ROME, at a time when he was so busily employed (as BECCATELLI writes) *per opprimere li heretici & aiutare i cattolici*, PAUL IV. renounced perhaps the zealous pontiff

pope's, without mentioning a syllable to Cardinal POLE, she dispatched orders to *Calais*, that no person coming from *Rome* should be suffered to pass the seas, and that all letters should be seized and sent to her; neither would she allow any notice to be taken of the new *cardinal legate*; she wrote also to her ambassador at *Rome* to tell the pope, as from herself, that " this was not the method to keep the " kingdom stedfast in the catholic faith, but ra- " ther to make it more heretical than ever, for

---

pontiff for the wiser politician, in which character he thought himself at liberty to dissemble with both the queen's emissaries and POLE's, and not explain the true reason of his present conduct. But he knew, from a long intimacy with the cardinal, that *he* had ever acted as the servile tool of the emperor, and his son, with whom he was then at war; that *he* had concurred with the queen in consenting to engage in PHILIP's present quarrels against him; that he had reason to suspect *he* would be constantly dabbling with the *French* ministers, to endeavour to bring HENRY II. off from his alliance with him; and had also very lately discovered upon the death of GARDINER, that the queen had pitched upon him for her CHANCELLOR as well as LEGATE, upon which POLE sifted the pope's sentiments by means of his confident, the ABBE DI SAN SALUTE, and PAUL found it necessary to order MORONE to dehort him from it, in the following letter.

" S. santità subito mi commise, non voleva per niente che
" quella pigliasse tel uffitio; il quale, dice, saria di carico al
" grado de cardinalato, & della legazione, & della particolar
" persona & qualità di V. S. reverendissima, & ch'io le facessi
" saper questa mente sua." C. Morone al C. Polo, Quirini, vol. v. let. XLVII.

" that

" that Cardinal POLE was the very *anchor* of the
" catholic party." She desired therefore, that HIS
" HOLINESS would be less precipitate in his proceed-
" ings, as she would charge him before God with
" all the evils that might ensue." To which, when
the pope made answer, " that he was recalled on
" some religious suspicions [m], HIS HOLINESS having
" cause

---

[m] Paul IV's character was of that cast, that, altho' he was always revered and respected in his life, and thro' his weight and superiority of abilities, was advanced to the popedom against the strongest resistance of the Imperial interest in the conclave, yet he was sure (from the natural timidity of mankind, too apt to insult those virtues they are no longer restrained by) to be spoken of with dislike and reproach after his death.

" He had a steady strictness of manners in himself, which
" made him despise all irresolute compliances in other men; he
" had a quick sense of injuries done him, and an austerity of
" temper which ill inclined him to forgive them, when done."

C. MORONE (who knew him better than PHILIPS's authority, GRATIANI, and felt his severities too harshly to flatter him) tells POLE;

" Nostro signore (Paolo IV.) ha un animo intrepido, riso-
" luto morir più tosto, che patir cosa che pare indegna del
" luoco che tiene." (Quirini, vol. v. let. 52.)

With such a *make* as this, it was impossible but the *intrepid* CARAFFA must *bear his faculties* somewhat loftier than the timid and irresolute POLE; and equally impossible, but that POLE should both dread and dislike CARAFFA. The austere *Theatine* had ever a jealous and watchful eye over the *wavering*

" cause to doubt his sincerity upon certain articles
" of the catholic faith," the queen replied by her
ambassador, " she presumed these suspicions must
" be of a very late date, otherwise HIS HOLINESS
" would not have been so warm in his encomiums
" upon him, when he took upon himself to *pro-
" pose* him in the consistory, for the *archbishoprick*
" of *Canterbury*; but if he was in any-wise cul-
" pable, or had given any just cause for such sus-
" picions since that time (which she could hardly
" credit) if HIS HOLINESS would please to communi-
" cate them to her, she would, in observance of the
" laws and privileges of her realm, refer them to
" the cognizance and decision of her own eccle-
" siastical courts; in doing which she would nei-
" ther suffer judgment to be impeded, nor the car-
" dinal to be undeservedly censured." a This proposal

---

legate of VITERBO, and so conscious was Pole known to be of this rigorous censor of his conduct, that some of his apologists have ascribed the severities he afterwards exercised in the discharge of his legatine function in ENGLAND, to his dread of so strict a master.

a BECCATELLI dwells principally upon those incidents in POLE's history, wherein he was concerned with the powers upon the continent, the emperor, the French king, the pope, or his consistory; those transactions came within the reach of his inquiries, and he seems to treat them with a more masterly pen; but that part of his history relative to his conduct in England he passes very lightly over, and appears to have been very superficially informed of the facts, either from his own knowlege,

CARDINAL REGINALD POLE. 117

posal of the queen's greatly embarrassed the POPE, who still persisted in declaring he had occasion for POLE's personal appearance at *Rome*, that he might confront him with Cardinal MORONE, whom he had imprisoned on the same suspicions of heresy. As soon as this affair came to be known to the legate, either in the whole or in part, apprehending the queen might have intercepted the pope's *brief of revocation*, as she had actually done; that he might get better information of the whole transaction, and not appear to act with contumacy and wilful

---

lege, or the instructions of others. These deficiencies have been greatly supplied by his *paraphrast* DUDITHIUS, who has inserted several intire SECTIONS either from his own better knowlege, or rather, I should suppose, by the addition of J. BAPTISTA BINARDI, POLE's *English secretary*, to whose correction he submitted his papers before he published them. From him T. PHILIPS has selected many incidents not mentioned by BECCATELLI; viz. POLE's being the sole instrument of reclaiming Sir JOHN CHEEK " by his Christian condescension," (vol. ii. p. 162.)—" and the repeated essays he made to recall " CRANMER to the paths of truth," p. 147. This latter story I have made some remarks upon in a former note. The merit of reclaiming poor Sir JOHN CHEEK (if driving a man to madness be *reclaiming* him) PRIULI, in a letter to BECCATELLI, had before given to Dr. FECKENHAM, the new abbot of *Westminster*.

" Detto il CIRCO che fu ministro d'Edoardo, e per tal causa
" in quei tempi favoratissimo, e anco maestro di tutti i giovani
" nobili, per opera di questo buon ABBATE, si e ravveduto,
" pentito, e rivocato da'suoi errori."—(Alvife Priuli a Monsig. Beccatelli—da Londra, Quirini, vol. v. 15 Dec. 1556.)

I 3 oppo-

opposition against the supreme head of the church, he dispatched N. ORMANET, a *Venetian*, and his holiness's *datary* ° in ENGLAND, who knew the temper of the court of *Rome*, with orders to throw himself at his holiness's feet, and know his final commands, which he should be ready to submit to as soon as known.

ORMANET [p] arrived at *Rome* in *August*, and laid the cardinal's business before the pope, assuring him of POLE's implicit obedience to whatever he should command. The pope received him with much appearance of courtesy; and, because of the

---

° A *datary* is an officer in the court of ROME, or acting under the pope's commission in other kingdoms, thro' whose hands all petitions for benefices must necessarily pass, to which he adds the date in these terms. *Datum apud*, &c.—from whence he has his title. Collier's Dict.

[p] T. PHILIPS says (vol. ii. p. 190.) "ORMANET told "BECCATELLI, that PAUL IV. cleared POLE from all suspi- "cion of heresy at this interview, saying, such rumours were "spread by malice and envy, which, as he had not spared the "most innocent author of Christianity, it was no matter of sur- "prise, if they attacked his followers."

I must beg leave to assure T. PHILIPS, that ORMANET did not tell BECCATELLI any such thing, neither does the latter give the least hint of any such tale; but DUDITHIUS picked up this story from some of Pole's domestics, and inserted it in his work; and T. PHILIPS, not giving himself the trouble to compare the *original* with the *paraphrast*, imputes it to the former at a venture.

ill

ill news he had lately heard of the defeat of his allies the *French* at ST. QUINTIN, where the CONSTABLE was taken prisoner, and also of the loss his own troops had suffered from the *Spanish* forces under the walls of *Anagni* in the CAMPANIA, he dropped [q] his former resentment both against King PHILIP and the CARDINAL, and temporized [r] for a time,

---

[q] POLE's letter of remonstrance (which he sent to PAUL IV. by ORMANET, 25 May 1557, who delivered it in August following) is penn'd with great submission, and artfully couches all his own resentment under the displeasure of the nobility and clergy of ENGLAND upon being deprived of their legate; his personal services in that office he left to be pleaded by ORMANET himself, who would not fail to acquaint his holiness, in how *mighty* a manner both his master and himself had exerted their zeal against the LUTHERANS both *living* and *dead*, at his visitations of the two universities under the lord cardinal's commission; where they had trampled on the poor bones of BUCER and FAGIUS, and ordered the dean of St. FRIDESWYDE "to dig up the heretical relics of BUCER's wife, and "not suffer them to lie near the hallowed remains of that "chaste and pious SAINT,"—' così in questo, come in tutte ' altre cose pertinenti alla legatione *navavit egregiam operam*.' Priuli Let. a Beccatelli, Quirini, vol. v.)

[r] T. PHILIPS leaves the final decision of this affair between the pope and his LEGATE, as a point undetermined in history, and thinks it sufficient to conclude his account, with saying, from DUTITHIUS, "That the pope dissembled his resent-" "ment;"—but his dissembling his resentment in 1557, just after the battle of ST. QUINTIN, proves nothing, since it appears from POLE's letter to PAUL IV. 30th March 1558, "That his legatine office continued still suspended, neither

a time, till he came to a resolution of offering terms of accommodation by Cardinal CARAFFA, his nephew, whom he sent in quality of legate to PHILIP: " to whose management (he said) he " would refer all disputes both with that prince " and C. POLE."

THE cardinal was therefore perfectly at ease with regard to his own situation; but the melancholy posture of public affairs greatly afflicted him, war raging on all sides, both by sea and land, between *England* and *France*, with the fatal loss of *Calais**, and

---

" could the queen or her parliament prevail to have it restored." Our English historians must therefore be in the wrong, when they say ' The restoration of POLE's legatine character ' was a *secret article* of the treaty with PHILIP,' (Rapin, vol. ii. p. 47.) GRATIANI's account seems most probable, ' that the ' further hearing was postponed by the interest of the queen,' and, as POLE died in the same year, it was never intirely cleared up in his favour, as the candid writer last-mentioned professedly acknowleges.

* The late inauspicious victory at ST. QUINTIN (which was gained by the assistance of the ENGLISH forces, whom MARY, in compliance with her husband, contrary to her matrimonial engagement to her subjects, against the faith of treaties, the sense of her best counsellors, and to the plunder and famine of her people, had *driven* into the field) was visited upon her in few months after, by the fatal loss of CALAIS, which the kings of ENGLAND had held fast, as the *master-key to the continent*, for more than 200 years, and which, but for a council of

CARDINAL REGINALD POLE. 121

and other towns in PICARDY; above all, the increasing indisposition of the queen, both in mind, and body, added to his uneasiness, who was herself deeply affected with the calamities of the war, and the absence of the king her husband, who was engaged in *Flanders*, and exposed his person to all the hazards of it. Upon the news, which was brought her from *Spain*, of the death of the late emperor, her father-in-law, [t] CHARLES V. who died Sep-

---

of misguided enthusiasts, with POLE and HEATH at their head, employed in forging racks and gibbets for their poor countrymen, instead of honourable weapons for the defence of their garrisons, might still have been kept by the same true English fortitude by which EDWARD III. first won it.

[t] T. PHILIPS has produced two quotations from the HOLY WRITINGS (vol. ii. p. 206.) to prove Charles V. to have been *a fool*. He was just such *a fool*, or rather, to give him his due honour, such an *illustrious madman*, as THE GREAT ALEXANDER.

He was born the same year with T. PHILIPS's hero, Cardinal POLE, but his STAR had so much the *ascendant* over the inferior lustre of his cotemporary's, that POLE dreaded, courted, and almost idolized him, to soothe him to his purpose.

This IMPERIAL *fool* had also too much *wisdom* to be seduced from the true interests of his crown by the insidious policy of ROME and her consistory; had too much *magnanimity* to take part in her bloody resentments against an insulted and *proscribed* sovereign; and had too much *christianity* to make peace with the natural enemies of the *Cross*, the worshippers of MAHOMET, at POLE's repeated instigation, that he might execute the menaces of the triple crown, and drench his sword in the blood of Christian princes and people.

tember

tember 21, 1558, she fell into a lingering fever, occasioned by a dropsical habit, that had once given her reason to believe she was with child, which continued * increasing upon her daily to the hour of her death.

To add to the national calamities, it pleased God to afflict Cardinal POLE about the same time with a violent ague, which harrassed him with very

---

* The French embassador marked with a very penetrating eye the chagrin which preyed upon the queen the two last years of her life, and paints her as the very picture of despair, in a letter to his master:

La dite Dame a mandée toute sa garde, ne se laissant voir en sa chambre que a quatre femmes; celle qui couche avec elle pour la cinquième, ne l'approche que trois ou quatre heures de nuit, que cette pauvre princesse demeure seulement couchée; le reste de son temps est tout emploié en pleurs, regrets, & en ecritures pour attirer son mari, & EN COLERE CONTRE SES SUJETS.

Let me subjoin to this, as a proper contrast to the false and fulsome eulogy which T. PHILIPS has given of MARY and her reign, this strong and spirited period with which Mr. CARTE closes the annals of her time:

"Every dreary year of her inglorious reign was blackened
"by remarkable disasters, and by such acts of injustice, ra-
"pine, violence, oppression, and tyranny, as Spanish councils
"only could have suggested; and having reduced the nation
"to the brink of ruin, she left it, by her seasonable decease,
"to be restored by her admirable successor to its ancient pro-
"sperity and glory." (Carte's Reign of Q. Mary.)

little

little intermission; and, being sensible of his approaching end, he set about the regulation of his temporal and eternal concerns, with his wonted calmness and confidence in the divine mercy, without the least alarm on the prospect of his dissolution. He expressed in his *will* [w], which he then made, great reverence and pious affection for the pope and the apostolic see, tho' he had been lately treated by the former with great severity; and that he might make the best provision in his power, out of the moderate reserve he had made, for his *Italian* friends who had followed his fortunes for many years, he left the management and administration of his effects [x] to ALVISE PRIULI, a *Venetian* gentleman [y], his dear friend, who knew every sentiment

---

[w] A copy of the cardinal's WILL written in Latin, and executed October 4th, 1558, about six weeks before his death, is printed—Ex Codice MSS. Bibliothecæ Ambrosianæ—in the Vth vol. Quirini, p. 181, from whence T. PHILIPS quoted it, though he has given a false reference, and pretends to have copied from the original MS. (vol. ii. p. 211.)

[x] Archbishop PARKER, POLE's successor, says, "He disposed of all his wealth in favour of the foreigners who came with him into ENGLAND." He seems, by the disposition of his will, to have had a view to this, by leaving his whole effects to the sole uncontroulable disposal of his VENETIAN friend PRIULI.

[y] I took notice before, in the course of these notes, that BECCATELLI always speaks of his very intimate friend PRIULI,

timent of his heart, and whom he loved with the affection of a brother, for his benevolence, learning, and faithful attachment to him. In remembrance of which he intreated his acceptance of a principal part of his fortune; but could not prevail with him to take it. PRIULI excused himself, saying, "He had followed him for the sake of "higher attainments, of which he had already "shared an ample proportion;" so that, altho' he was left sole heir by the cardinal's will, he would accept of nothing but his *Breviary* and *Diurnal*, books constantly used by his friend at his daily devotions. This PRIULI [a] is the same person whom I men-

---

ULI, as he does here, under the simple appellation of *Gentiluomo Veniziano*, and not as a NOBLE VENETIAN, I therefore supposed it must have been a mistake to call him LORD PRIULI, as POLE's biographer often does; but I must acknowlege, notwithstanding BECCATELLI's authority, that the cardinal speaks of him in his WILL as being "PATRICIUM VENE-"TUM, meum intimum amicum." Quirini, vol. v. p. 183.

[a] PRIULI writes a very tender and affecting letter to the archbishop BECCATELLI at his see of RAGUSA (dated London, June 13, 1559) on the loss of their common friend C. POLE, whose death had so afflicted and disordered him, that he was not able to sit down sooner to write on so mournful a subject: from this letter I think we may date our author's first design of compiling the present MEMOIRS of the cardinal's life, which he was probably solicited to undertake by PRIULI himself, who engaged to supply him with materials for such a work from the cardinal's letters and papers, which, he hints to his friend

in

CARDINAL REGINALD POLE.

I mentioned in the beginning of this history to have entered into so strict a friendship with REGINALD POLE at PADUA, in 1532, that he would never leave him afterwards, attending him in all his travels, during his several embassies and legations; and notwithstanding many honourable preferments were offered him both at ROME and in his native country, he slighted them all, rather than forsake a companion he was so much attached to. And when the states of VENICE had interceded with

---

in the course of this Italian letter, he intended should appear to the world in some form or other, for the honour of the writer, and the edification of mankind.

These "Monimenti pretiosissimi dell' ingegno, & della pieta" his proposal was to carry with him to RAGUSA, as soon as his health and executorship would permit him to leave ENGLAND.

"Con speranza, che ne possa venire non solo vera e perpetua laude a lui, con gloria di Dio, ed edificazione non solo di questa sua patria, ma del resto della Christianità."

Et chi sà che la divina Providenza non m'aprà, un dì, la via di poter mettere in esecuzione questo mio disegno?

From these passages I would venture to conjecture, if Priuli lived to see his friend either at VENICE or RAGUSA, he might leave these monuments in his hands, of which BECCATELLI might presume he should make the best use in his power, and fulfil the pious wish of PRIULI (who died within seven or eight months after he left ENGLAND) if he extracted from them, together with what his own long intercourse with POLE would supply, such an *historical panegyric* to his memory as we have here before us.

JULIUS

Julius III. to make him the reversionary grant of the bishoprick of BRESCIA on a future vacancy, when Cardinal DURANTE [a] was promoted to it; it was with much difficulty they could persuade him to accept it, so desirous was he of always continuing one of C. Pole's family, which in effect he never relinquished, preferring that situation to all the riches and honours in the world.

AFTER the cardinal's death, during the [b] xx months in which he survived him, his whole attention

---

[a] Cardinal DURANTE was one of POLE's intimates, as appears by an *Italian* letter to him at BRESCIA from the English Cardinal during his retirement at MAGUZANO in 1553.

DURANTE died 1558, but PAUL IV. revoked the grant of JULIUS III, and *provided* some other person to the bishoprick of BRESCIA, which the philosophic PRIULI bore with his wonted calmness, thus speaking of it in a letter to BECCATELLI at RAGUSA:

"Io mi trovo tanto piu contento, essendo fuori del pericolo d'aver a sostenere un di peso molto più grave che non comporteria la debolezza delle mie forze, per la rivocatione degli *accessi*, che V. S. averà deja inteso."
 A Monsignor L. Beccatelli, da Londra, alli 15 Dec^e 1556.
(Quirini, vol. v.)

[b] The very amiable character of POLE's last and dearest friend ALVISE PRIULI, may excite the curiosity of the reader to follow him with his eye to his last stage: He left ENGLAND Nov. 6, 1559, in a very declining state of health (as we are told in an *Italian* letter to BECCATELLI, dated PARIS, December

CARDINAL REGINALD POLE.   127

tention was taken up in executing his laſt *will* with the moſt ſcrupulous exactneſs, and taking indefatigable pains to collect together his effects which lay ſcattered in different places; which he diſpoſed of with the ſtricteſt punctuality, as he judged moſt anſwerable to his friend's inclination.

When the cardinal had executed his *will*, and acquitted himſelf of all his wordly ᶜ affairs, he bent

---

ber 30, 1559). He propoſed going ſoon to Orleans for the reſt of the winter, intending, if poſſible, to ſee Italy in the ſpring; but as he died about the July following, he might perhaps only reach Venice, to die there, and expire in the arms of his chief ſurviving friend the archbiſhop of Ragusa, whom he had deſired to meet at that place.

And yet, not all this natural benevolence of temper, embelliſhed by polite literature, and harmoniſed by the intercourſe and ſociety of the good and great men of his time, could ſave the ſpirit of Priuli from being tinctured with the baneful and bloody principles of the church in which he was nurſed. He talks of " burning heretics alive" with all the compoſure of an inquiſitor; and relates the barbarous ſcene " where they compelled the pitiable and almoſt inſane Sir J. " Cheek to harangue his tortured countrymen at the ſtake, " and preach up his own converſion to them for their convic- " tion, as they lay bound in expectation of the flames," with all the inſenſibility of a Bonner.

  Lettere a L. Beccatelli, Quirini. vol. v. p. 345. Appendix.

ᶜ One of the laſt acts of the cardinal's life, with reſpect to worldly affairs, was, the letter he directed to the Princeſs
Eliza-

bent his thoughts solely upon God, and received the rites and sacraments of the Romish church in their usual course; and, weak as he was, heard mass every day; and, upon the *elevation of the host*, he ordered himself to be raised up in his bed, and was supported upon his knees by two gentlemen of

---

ELIZABETH (if his death happened, as his Italian biographer says, xv NOVEMBER) the very day before he died.

It is dated *Lambeth Palace, November* 14, and was sent by HOLLAND his chaplain, dean of WORCESTER, as it should seem, to bespeak her favour to his memory, or at least to exculpate himself from any share in the severities she had suffered under the lash of popish malevolence.

The publishers of the fifth volume of POLE's letters, not being better informed, will have it to be written to Q. Mary, not considering both the impropriety in point of time of addressing himself to a dying queen, and also the absurdity of supposing POLE could be under a necessity of writing an apology for himself to MARY, to whom all his actions stood perfectly well approved—But the BRESCIAN librarians were so fond of any relick of POLE's, that they never inquired into the merit of it, but took the pains to procure, from J. BERGENTINI, an *Italian* translation of it, lest foreigners should be unacquainted with so valuable a curiosity—They may *now* have the pleasure of reading (in the fifth volume of Quirini, p. 276.) that POLE thought himself obliged to explain his conduct not to the world only, but

" particolarmente a M. V. che la Divina Providentia ha
" exaltata a si alto honore & dignità." more especially
" to the Princess ELIZABETH " being of that honour and dig-
" nity, that the Providence of God hath called you unto."
(Pole's original words).

his

his chamber. He had the *Holy Scriptures* and other devout books frequently read to him, which seemed to give him a sensible relief even in the paroxysms of his fever. The day before he died he begged to receive the *last unction*, with as much calmness as if he had been in full health, and spoke very distinctly to his last moments. It was a remarkable event, that the queen and POLE should expire the same day, her majesty dying on the 15th of November in the morning, and the cardinal about *nine* the same evening, at the distance of but XVI hours. He had been told of the queen's death, as he never ceased enquiring about her almost every instant, and would not suffer any one to attempt to deceive him; and when the account [d] was brought him, he

---

[d] This accidental circumstance, of C. POLE's dying on the same day with the QUEEN, was probably a very desireable event to himself, a man naturally of a timorous and apprehensive temper, which long sickness must have weakened still more—He might dread the thought of being sent back to his austere master PAUL IV, from whom he had much more reason to fear ill treatment than from ELIZABETH, who was generous enough to continue two more violent men than himself, HEATH and THIRLBY, of YORK and ELY, of her council, till they insulted her with their constant opposition, and obstructed every necessary measure for the establishment of her government, but they were neither *bound to stakes*, nor *cast into dungeons*.

The Roman catholic writers, DUDITHIUS (as he then was) GRATIANI, and PHILIPS (who, contrary to the Levitical prohibition, is a great *observer of times*) have delivered down this contingency,

he said, 'I hope Christ, in his mercy, will not abandon this poor kingdom;' neither did this event the least alter or discompose him, but he continued in prayer and devout meditation, with great firmness of mind to the last. About an hour before he expired (as I was told by the bishop of ST. ASAPH, who gave him *extreme unction*, and was always in the room with him) he asked, if the book of *Recommendatory Prayers*, to be used at the soul's departure, was ready, as he had desired; which when the bishop ⁸ shewed him, he looked upon it, and said, 'Now then is the time to use it,' and with these words he expired, and was received, we hope, into the habitations of *Blessed Spirits*, with

---

contingency, of their dying about the same time, as an extraordinary interposition of Providence: and Dr. COLE, in his *Funeral Oration*, seems to make too familiar an allusion, when he applies to them the passage in SAMUEL, ch. i.—" They were " lovely in their lives, and in their deaths they were not di- " vided"——

(Oratio habita in funere C. POLI, QUIRINI, vol. v.)

⁸ This bishop of ST. ASAPH was THOMAS GOLDWELL, who had been bred up in the austere discipline of PAUL IV. the founder of the order of *Theatines*; to a convent of which order at RAVENNA he retired the year after Pole's decease: there Mr. ADDISON saw his picture (anno 1700) with this *not very humble* inscription:

Thomas Goldwellus, Ep. Aſˢ Tridⁿᵒ Concilio contra Hæreticos, & in Angliâ contra Elisabet. Fidei Confessor conspicuus——

(Addison's Travels, 12mo, p. 93.)

the

Cardinal REGINALD POLE. 131

the pious and catholic queen, his mistress, after a toilsome pilgrimage of FIFTY-EIGHT YEARS AND SIX MONTHS.

HIS body, according to the custom of ENGLAND, lay in state 40 days, in the palace where he died, being inclosed in a leaden coffin, and raised upon a stage erected for that purpose in the middle of a large hall hung round with black, before which four masses were sung each day, a ceremony usually performed at the obsequies of the nobility, and persons of distinction in that kingdom; at the expiration of which time, a sumptuous herse was prepared to receive it, from whence it was conducted in great funeral pomp to the metropolitan church of CANTERBURY [f], which is distant from LONDON

---

[f] The funeral oration, spoken to the clergy of the diocese of CANTERBURY on the loss of their archbishop, is a curious specimen of the style of composition in that age, whose orators had now laid aside their CICERO, and their TACITUS, to take up the *Vulgate* in obedience to the TRENTINE fathers, who had stamped not only a religious, but even a CLASSICAL purity upon all its barbarisms. From this storehouse the oration I am speaking of has borrowed its principal ornaments:

" Talis erat post CHRISTUM, qualem describit ESAIAS."

" In bracchio suo nos, ut agnos, congrega*vit*, & in sinu
" suo leva*vit*, & fœtus ipse porta*vit*, pro nobis denique ora-
" *vit*, & vigila*vit*, tanquam rationem pro animabus nostris
" redditurus—Verus noster erat JACOB, quos tam tenerè, ut
" ille

LONDON about forty miles, where it was attended by the clergy of the diocefs, and depofited by his own direction in the chapel of St. Thomas.

Thus ended his life: after which I prefume it will not be thought unfeafonable to defcant a little on the diftinguifhing manners and qualities of fo eminent a character.

First, as to his perfon [a]:

He was of the middle ftature, and of a lean habit of body; he was fair, and yellow-hair'd, which is the ufual colour and complexion of his

---

" ille olim fuum Joseph, dilexit, qui nobis tunicam etiam
" polymitam, id eft, varietate bonorum operum contextam
" concinnavit."
    Oratio in funere habita Card. Poli, ex Cod. MSS. Vaticanis—Quirini, vol. v. p. 196.

[a] The admirers of T. Philips may perhaps like his picture of Cardinal Pole better than mine, which profeffes only to be as exact a copy as I could draw from my original Beccatelli. His indeed is no more, tho' he is not candid enough to own (thro' the whole xii fection) the mafters he was totally obliged to. Dudithius is indeed his principal guide, as being more copious than the Italian; but he feldom takes the leaft notice of either the one or the other (but in one half fentence, p. 225, note) thro' a chapter of above 20 pages of almoft a *verbal* tranflation.

country-

countrymen [b]. The oval of his face was rather large, but enlivened with an eye benign and chearful. His beard, when he was young, was of a very light colour; he had a healthful constitution, tho' not a strong one, and was seldom out of order but when he was troubled with a rheumatic defluxion, which fell sometimes into his arm, and was very painful to him; and at others occasioned an inflammation in one of his eyes. He was very temperate in eating; but being apt to suffer from indigestion, he was not able to bear much fasting: he allowed himself two meals a day, but the least was in the evening. He was no great sleeper, generally rising before day-break, to follow his studies and devotions: he did not like the parade of servants about him; but often went to bed, and arose in the morning without any attendants. He had

---

[b] Altho' it be not an easy matter to judge of a man's complexion and the colour of his hair from a print, and I have never seen the picture of C. POLE, which RAPHAEL D'URBIN did *not* paint, tho' RAPHAEL BORGHESE possibly might; yet I will venture to say, BECCATELLI, who was an ITALIAN (the natives of whose country are commonly of very *dark complexions* and *black hair*) meant to describe POLE as being *fair* and *yellow-hair'd*, very different from what his eye had been used to in Italy, which (as all historians take notice) is the colour of the natives of BRITAIN; his words are, " *di color trà bianco e rosso*," which T. PHILIPS has applied to his complexion instead of his hair, and translated, " his complexion was fair, mixed with an agreeable vermilion." (PHILIPS's Life of POLE, vol. ii. sect. 12.)

that-guard upon his conduct thro' every period of his life, that he had always the reputation of strict personal chastity both in ENGLAND and [c] abroad.

HE was not ambitious of great wealth, but was very liberal and charitable in the disposal of his revenues. He had a pleasure in seeing his table genteelly covered, but always managed with such œconomy, as to measure his expences by his income, which, till [d] *within the last year*, had been always very inconsiderable.

As

---

[c] The only reference T. PHILIPS has made to POLE's biographers thro' his last chapter, is to a line in DUDITHIUS, in confirmation of the cardinal's universal reputation, for *personal purity*. His virtue was probably untainted, tho' he did not escape the reproach of incontinence even in the conclave, from that *strict censor of manners*, the THEATINE cardinal, which imputation has since been fixed upon him by Archbishop PARKER. I acknowlege it my opinion, that his own masterly vindication of himself from the charge of the Cardinal CARAFFA will not suffer me to give credit to the aspersion.

" Quoniam vero nobis susceptum est, ut de illius *vitâ*, non
" de *laude* dicemus, ne *hoc* quidem reticendum putamus."
T. CASA, de BEMBO.

[d] The expression in the Italian, is " da l'ultimo anno in poi,' which should mean as I have rendered it; but I know not how to make sense of the passage, or reconcile these words to the truth of facts. It is notorious, that POLE enjoyed the revenues of the archbishopric, on CRANMER's suspension by PAUL IV. which by the *acta consistorialia* was Dec. 11th 1555.

His

As soon as he was made *a cardinal* he was deprived of every thing he had in ENGLAND; upon which pope PAUL III. appointed him a pension of 200 crowns a month, which he lived upon while he abode at ROME; when he was in a public character abroad, he supported himself out of the procurations and emoluments that were appendant to his legatine office. Upon the death of MAT. GIBERTI, bishop of VERONA, who had a great affection for him, and knew the straitness of his fortune, he received a bequest of 2,000 ducats *per annum* out of a pension that bishop enjoyed upon the see of GRANADA in SPAIN, with a power of *transferring* it; and also the [e] precentorship of VALENCIA, to the value of 800 ducats more.

His income must therefore have been almost as great then as when he was actually in possession of the see. I should therefore conjecture, as there are other errors in the impression, this must also be one. I should imagine then BECCATELLI wrote, 'dà l'ultimi anni in poi,' in the plural; which will mean, 'till within these few last years,' i. e. 'till his arrival in ENGLAND, and the consequent appointments made him.'

[e] The words in the original are "la *Capiscolia di Valencia*," the word *Capiscolia* is SPANISH, and means either *chantry*, or the office of *chanter* or *precentor*. The sense of the passage may be then, "He left him either *the precentorship* (as I have rendered it) or "a bequest of such a value payable out of the "*chantry* of VALENCIA:" which, tho' not so well express'd in the original, seems to be the truer meaning.

The emperor [f] likewise appointed him a pension of 2,000 ducats out of the revenues of the church of BURGOS; and at the death of the cardinal of RAVENNA, which happened in 1549, PAUL III. gave him the abbacy of GAVELLO in the diocess of ADRIA, rated at 1,000 crowns *per annum*. This was [g] his income till he returned to ENGLAND. PAUL III. who had a great value for him, would have promoted him to the bishopric of SPOLETO, as it was in the neighbourhood of ROME; but the cardinal, who thought himself obliged in quality of his post to reside at ROME, did not think the acceptance of a bishopric compatible with it, he

---

[f] T. PHILIPS's extreme wariness, in omitting to take notice of the pension POLE received from the emperor CHARLES V. altho' he has given a list of the rest, implies his suspicion left this bounty of CHARLES's might seem to have been given him, in reward of his former attachment to his interest, and as the purchase of his future services.

[g] There is a candour and ingenuousness in BECCATELLI's manner of telling his story, which scorns to disguise or conceal any thing; DUDITHIUS suppresses many things, and softens others, if they seem to affect his hero's dignity, or discredit his reputation; some of these peculiarities have already been noticed, it is very observable in the present case, that, notwithstanding BECCATELLI's catalogue of POLE's several pensions and bequests lay before him, he has not taken notice of one of them.—Let me add, that it appears from a fair computation of POLE's income, by BECCATELLI's list, that it did not amount to less than 3,000 *l. per annum*, at the lowest valuation, before he came to ENGLAND.

therefore

CARDINAL REGINALD POLE.

therefore modestly declined it, without giving offence to any one.

He went afterwards into England, as I have related, in 1554, where he was nominated by queen Mary to the see of Canterbury; but refused to accept it, till he had the pope's promise that he would never recall him from England. This petition he presented by the hands of Thomas Goldwell[h], bishop of St. Asaph; that he might,

---

[h] It is somewhat extraordinary, Pole should attempt such a stipulation as this a with pope of Paul IV's unpliant temper; and, if he did make it, it is as extraordinary that no mention should be made of it, and no thanks returned by Pole for such a concession, in his letter to the pope, wherein he acknowleges having received his *bull* of election to the see of Canterbury. (Quirini, vol. v. epist. 9.)

T. Philips, upon the strength of this passage in Beccatelli, asserts, in his usual vein of compliment to Pole's modest merits, that " on his return from banishment he declined, as much as in him lay, the see of Canterbury," vol. ii. p. 229. His waving the acceptance of it, if true, till he could secure a promise never to be recalled to Rome, was a step of *prudence* rather than *piety*, to shelter himself under the milder influence of Mary's favour, from the tempestuous rule of so rough a spirit as Paul's; but to have declined accepting an office, whose revenues he already enjoyed, would not have been to his honour; he would likewise have much embarrassed his mistress by his refusal, who would not easily have found another person with zeal enough to undertake so weighty an office, and leave all the emoluments of it to the enjoyment of her favourite the Legate.

with

with his holiness's permission, devote himself, without interruption, to the duties of his charge; whereupon he was ordained priest, and soon after consecrated archbishop of CANTERBURY.

THE revenues of that see were then about [a] 12,000 *crowns per annum*, over and above which the queen granted him a pension of 3,000 *ducats* yearly out of the bishopric [b] of WINCHESTER. His carriage in the exalted station to which he was now raised, was so modest and humble, that he never solicited the crown for any favours, not even for his own patrimony which he enjoyed before his attainder by HENRY VIII. He would not so much as petition

---

[a] GRATIANI, who seems to have copied from BECCATELLI or DUDITHIUS, speaks of the value of the archbishopric of CANTERBURY in POLE's time, as being full 30,000 crowns per annum. It is probable therefore there may be a mistake in the printing of our author in this place.

[b] Archbishop PARKER says, " POLE had the sequestration of the *whole* profits of the see of WINTON from GARDINER's death, till WHITE, who had been bred there, and had been master of the school and warden of the college, solicited a translation thither from LINCOLN, of which he was bishop, and obtained it upon the payment of 1000 *l.* yearly pension to the cardinal."

" Quæ conventio (says the archbishop) cum simoniam redoleret, utrique a papa, non sine remuneratione, absolvenda fuerat." Antiq. Eccl. Brit. p. 527.

for the [c] EARLDOM of WARWICK, which he had an hereditary claim to, and was much pressed by his friends to apply for.

I REMEMBER a circumstance that happened to him during his second LEGATION at the *Council* of TRENT; 4,000 ducats of his GRANADA-pension were brought to him there, which from some accident or other had been in arrear to him; but having supported himself so long without feeling the want of it, and kept clear of all debts by his usual good management, he very liberally divided the whole sum among his domestics and dependants in proportion to their stations, without regarding that he was but a poor cardinal himself, and at a great distance from home. But yet whenever he was called upon to make a splendid appearance, he ex-

---

[c] Foreigners, who know nothing of our laws of descents, and the great rights of *primogeniture* established in this kingdom, may be pardoned for talking of the cardinal's *hereditary claim* to the earldom of WARWICK; but it is ridiculous to hear T. PHILIPS assert, as he does (vol. ii. p. 228.) that " the " earldom of WARWICK was devolved to POLE by inherit-" ance."

Whereas by T. P's own supposition (tho' a false one) his eldest brother's son was still living; but however, he had *one* if not *two* elder brothers then alive, so that an *hereditary claim* to that title was impossible; yet as it was a family-title, tho' forfeited by the treason of his uncle, it is not improbable MARY would have revived it in him, if he had asked it.

erted

erted himself with a becoming dignity, and [d] shewed a princely magnificence of spirit, which he inherited as his birth-right.

He was of a very meek and mild disposition, which some were apt to construe pusillanimity; but he, who had the pattern of his blessed Master always before him, neither opposed [e], nor resented injuries.

He was very facetious and entertaining in conversation, of which his great knowlege of the world, and extensive reading, supplied him with a very

---

[d] This is very handsomely spoken by BECCATELLI, and may be thought not inadequate to his patron's merits; but T. PHILIPS hath taken a much higher flight, and exerted *the true sublime of nonsense* in displaying his idea of the cardinal's munificence.

" His bounty, like the sun, spread its ray, and shone away
" the superfluity."
Philips's Life of Pole, vol. ii. p. 227.

[e] When POLE was basking in the sun-shine of royal favour, and felt the happiness of ease and greatness too sensibly to chuse to have them ruffled by altercations and dissentions, he bore the reproaches of PAUL IV. with great composure, and desired nothing more than to keep out of his reach; but he did no always practise these condescending virtues; the *Publisher* of the book *De Unitate* &c.—the *Apologist* to CHARLES V.—and the *Author* of the letter to EDWARD VI. can never be said with truth, " neither to have opposed, nor resented injuries."

pleasing

Cardinal REGINALD POLE.

pleasing and inexhaustible fund; I never knew a person who had such ready wit, and so many apposite allusions in his common discourse, as himself; they seemed to flow from him without the least conceit or affectation, and even diffuse themselves very pertinently thro' most of his writings. I will give [f] a few specimens of this talent of his, which have not yet slipt my memory.

---

[f] BECCATELLI seems to have imitated PLUTARCH's *manner*, in the two lives he has written of those intimate friends and cotemporary cardinals, CONTARINI and POLE. Like him he has dwelt more upon the *minutiæ* of their characters, and those little distinguishing *peculiarities*, which PLUTARCH calls τα της ψυχης σημεια, 'the indexes of the heart,' than upon the greater features of their conduct. In this imitation he seems also to have fallen into the very fault of his original, "the dwelling too long on these trifles;" which, if pleasing to a certain degree, in the *excess* become loathsome and ridiculous. Dr. *Middleton*'s criticism upon PLUTARCH's *Life* of CICERO is justly applicable to BECCATELLI's work before us.

"He huddles over his greater acts in a summary manner, and dwells upon his dreams and *jests*."
Preface to the Life of Cicero.

The graver manners of CONTARINI were not indeed so pregnant with these mirthful sallies as the more courteous disposition of POLE, which makes the life of that cardinal, in that respect, the more preferable: the utmost merit one can give BECCATELLI, in acknowlegement of the latter part of this work, is, "that he has trifled at least as *ingeniously* as PLUTARCH;" and the utmost praise one can allow POLE, in honour of the following witticisms, is "that he is to the full as good a jester as CICERO."

I REMEMBER he was talking one day of a bishop, a friend of his, who resided chiefly at *Rome* himself, tho' he had censured others for doing so:

"He's very excusable," says he, "he only eats garlic himself, that he may bear the smell of it when he is in company with those who love it."

SPEAKING, at another time, of a young man of parts, who was too forward in giving his opinion in conversation, he said, "Learning in young heads is like new wine, which frets and ferments for a time; but refines and settles by degrees, and comes at length to its full strength."

A PERSON, who pretended to great skill in astrology, told him, "He had calculated his nativity, and foresaw great things for him." "Possibly," said the cardinal, "but you don't consider I have had a second birth (meaning *baptism*) which has obscured all the influence of the first."

A CONVERSATION [s] arising upon the study of the scriptures, when one person said, "They ought to be

---

[s] It is the duty of a translator to follow his author step by step, and it is his own fault if he has chosen a bad master; but one would wonder what could tempt POLE's *late* BIOGRAPHER to string every bawble he could find in BECCATELLI to deck

"be one's sole employment," and another replied, "Well, but other studies may be called in as "*hand-maids.*" "Know ye not (says the cardinal) that the *hand-maid* AGAR was cast out?"

I WAS present another time, when a bishop, who was very intimate in his family, and whom he had often rebuked for staying too much in ROME, and neglecting his diocess, came to take leave of him, and told him, "He was going to reside at his see "for a month, that his lordship might not rebuke "him any more." "Well, Sir," says the cardinal, "it will be some satisfaction to me to think "your punishment will be somewhat less for "this"[a] — *vapulabis minus.*

UPON

---

deck out his history, and at the same time keep to himself the honour of having collected them.

The whole merit of these *impromptu's* depends solely on the quickness of the repartee, or the aptitude of the application; and they are perhaps the dullest things in the world, when retailed out, one after another, without any leading incident to introduce or recommend them.

[a] It has been remarked by C. Quirini, and was the admiration of some of POLE's great partizans among his cotemporaries, that he was most conversant in the sacred scriptures, and most happy in the application of them on all occasions, of any man of his time. Perhaps a nice judge, both of composition and conversation, would blame him for employing this talent to a faulty excess, if he should enter into a critical examination

Upon reading a letter of condolence to a nobleman upon the death of a near relation, which was filled with strange conceits, and extravagant flights of rhetoric, "It is the very best letter for the pur- "pose," says he, "I ever beheld; for it will be "impossible to read it without laughing."

Being desired to go and hear a preacher of some note, who plumed [b] himself somewhat too vainly upon his talents for the pulpit, when he was asked his opinion of him, "He acquits himself very "well," said the cardinal, "but he should preach "first to himself."

A gentleman who had just planted a very pretty vineyard near Rome, and desired him to come and see it; and said, as he took his leave, "He hoped "for the honour of seeing him there again 30 "years hence, and he would then see it greatly

---

mination of his *Familiar Letters*; in many of which these beauties, if they are such, are rather too predominant. He seems also to have been so diligent a student in the Latin vulgate, that he has tinctured, and I may say debased the style of his *latter* compositions in general, by too indiscriminate a use of it; and we may see, that not only his dispatches, his letters of business and of compliment, his orations and his invectives, but even his jokes, his very *Concetti*, speak the language of the Latin vulgate.

[b] The expression in the Italian is very elegant and expressive, '*sul pulpito si pavoneggieva*,' *had all the pride of a peacock in his pulpit.*

"improved."

"improved." "What offence have I given you," replied the cardinal, "that you should wish me to be so long an exile from my own *true* country? Indeed, Sir, I don't thank you for your invitation."

When he was in [c] Flanders, and had waited two days for an audience of the emperor, the bishop of Aras made an apology to him for his having been detained so long on account of his Imperial majesty's being indisposed. "I own," said the cardinal, "I was a little surprised, that I, who have access to God every day in behalf of the emperor, should find it so difficult to gain admittance once of the emperor in the cause of God."

Talking one day of a gentleman, who was very finical in the care of his beard, which cost him, it was said, 3 *crowns* a month: "At this rate," said Pole, "the beard is of more worth than the head."

---

[c] Dudithius, and T. Philips from him, have recorded another *bon mot* of Pole's, not mentioned by Beccatelli, which seems to have more of vanity than prudence in it.

A courier being intercepted on the road, who was bringing him some dispatches, and the people about him expressing some concern on the occasion, he said, "It was an accident rather to be wished than lamented."

"Optandum enim mihi esset potius evenire, ut quæ a me geruntur, palam fierent omnia." Vita Poli.

He was very quick at such smart and lively repartees as these, which are still in the memories of his familiar acquaintance.

He was likewise very sincere in his friendships, and an utter enemy to flattery [d] and falsehood; but

---

[d] T. Phillips mentions Pole's behaviour with regard to Gardiner "as a noble testimony of his Christian forbearance, and abhorrence of resentment, both during his lifetime, and after his death." An impartial reader of our history will be very apt to dissent from this opinion, and discover strong marks of pusillanimity in Pole's passive compliances to him when they acted together; and also of unbecoming flattery to his memory when dead.

The French embassador observed with much dislike the *first* in many of his letters;—His own letter to Philip, when Gardiner was dying, and his compliment to his extraordinary virtues when dead, in his letter to the university of Cambridge, are very strong impeachments of his veracity.

Hoc tantum dicam quod jam sensimus, quasi simul cum illo (Gardiner) Religio & Justitia laborarent.
Card. Polus, Regi Philippo Ep. xxii. Quirini, vol. v.

And, in his letter of thanks to the university of Cambridge on their appointing him chancellor in Gardiner's room,

He writes it as his opinion,

"That two persons (speaking of Fisher and Gardiner) could not be named in the whole Kingdom, in whom the Supreme Being had given a clearer evidence of his *mercy* towards this country."
Philips's Life of C. Pole, vol. ii. p. 171.

gave

gave his opinion on all occasions with such a graceful propriety, that, tho' he dissented from others, he did it without giving offence. I have heard his brother-cardinals remark, that when he gave his vote in the consistory on any debate, he spake with that modest freedom, as never to disoblige; which could be said of few, or perhaps of nobody, but himself.

He ᵉ had so much forgiveness of temper, that when *two* Englishmen, who came post from Eng-

---

ᵉ Beccatelli relates these two stories greatly to the honour of Pole, and if they had been as he has represented them, they would have been convincing proofs of great nobleness of mind; but it is evident from the strictest examination of the suspected Parties (as recorded in four Italian letters printed by Quirini, vol. iii. from MSS. in the Cervini family) that, though the circumstances against them were suspicious, there was not sufficient evidence to convict them.

Although Henry's provocations were great, and he had a people ready to have executed his most vindictive commands, in whose country it is not even now deemed an unbecoming resentment to buy the blood of an enemy at the hand of an assassin, yet Beccatelli, who never palliates or disguises any thing, nor advances what he does not believe himself, does not once accuse Henry VIII. as being the instigator of either of these plots.

Dudithius has indeed extended the crime to the king of England in his paraphrase, and T. Phillips has retailed it from him with the additional infusion of his own wonted acrimony

ENGLAND to aſſaſſinate him whilſt he was at CAPRANICA, were taken up, and confeſſed their deſign, he would not ſuffer them to be executed, but ſaid, "As the injury was perſonally to himſelf, "he inſiſted he might have the privilege of ſparing their lives," and they were accordingly ſent to the gallies for a ſhort time.

I WAS told alſo [f] by a perſon who was preſent, that after he was ſettled in ENGLAND, when he heard the reproach of hereſy which was imputed to him by Pope PAUL IV. and had drawn up an apology in his own vindication, in which he had retorted ſome things pretty ſeverely on the pope, he gave his papers to his ſecretary, that they might be fairly tranſcribed; and when they were brought to him afterwards, ſheet by ſheet, for his reviſal, he read them over as he ſtood by the fire, and repeating theſe words, "*non revelabis pudenda patris tui,*" he threw them into the flames.

SUCH was the amiable ſweetneſs of his temper which abhorred the gratification of revenge—his unbounded charity comprehended all mankind, and extended itſelf alike to all. And under his own

---

mony againſt HENRY—But neither the *original* author, nor the *original* letters of evidence, once mention the king of ENGLAND as the encourager of theſe ſuppoſed aſſaſſins.

[f] Dudithius has choſen to omit this ſtory.

CARDINAL REGINALD POLE. 149

roof, the meanest servants of his houshold were the objects of his care, and in case of sickness he frequently visited them in person. This Christian benevolence [a] of heart made him sometimes liable to be imposed upon by bad men, who palmed themselves upon him as *poor scholars*, or persons of extraordinary piety, characters that had great weight

---

[a] Beccatelli, who had an affectionate attachment to both his masters, whose memories he has celebrated, and knew the distinguishing features of their characters, seems to have ascribed *philantbropy* to POLE, and to have been perhaps more strongly attached to him for that endearing quality. Such indeed appears to have been the original cast of his natural disposition, till he attempted to graff another passion upon it, RELIGIOUS ENTHUSIASM, whose incompatible opposition to the true spirit of the former, occasioned all the future contrarieties which distracted his character, and which neither he himself, nor all his admirers since, can ever reconcile.

Hence it was that he insulted, vilified, and proscribed his king, whom he still professed to love, and to whom he acknowleged irrefragable obligations: hence it was, that he travelled over Europe to instigate the Christian powers to invade and distress his native country, to which he acknowleged at the same time the most filial duty and reverence. Hence he sacrificed his parent, relations, and friends, to an indiscreet obedience to the papal authority; and gloried in their fall as martyrs to his own enthusiasm; and when he returned triumphant to his mother country, he suffered the most inhuman tortures to be exercised on a people he pretended to love; and vowed the most passionate desire for the happiness of poor *Cranmer*, though he consented to let him expire under the most shocking of human punishments.

with him; altho' impostures of this kind are too common in the world, many men concealing very base principles under the garb of great outward sanctity: his indulgence to men of such pretensions exposed him to the censure of some people who are more forward to find a fault than to excuse one. His wish was to be serviceable to all, and if he found any one who had fallen into erroneous opinions, he strove by lenient methods to lead him out of them, and not drive him to despair by the harshness of his rebukes; saying, that all but obstinate and notorious [a] reprobates had a title to mild and gentle treatment. These were the arts he used with his old favourite friend [b] M. ANTONIO FLAMINIO,

---

[a] This, I suppose, is the salvo, under which the Romanists shelter their doctrine of persecution. 'Tis but pronouncing the poor heretic *" ostinato & publico,"* and then leading him away to the stake without further remorse.

[b] T. PHILIPS, with his usual bitterness, aggravates Beccatelli's expressions, and adds to his account of Flaminio's " having imbibed *alcune opinioni non molto sicure*, from the conversation of VALDES," that he returned to Rome *a proselyte to his impious system* (vol. i. p. 300.)

Let us examine a little into the merits of this favourite convert of POLE's; a story not mentioned by DUDITHIUS, but much dwelt upon by C. QUIRINI, and from him by T. PHILIPS.

C. QUIRINI, writing in vindication of the *Society of Viterbo*, (Præfatio, vol. iii. pars 2da) presumes he has established the orthodoxy

CARDINAL REGINALD POLE.

FLAMINIO, who had spent some time at NAPLES, where he had imbibed some dangerous notions from the conversation of VALDES; in order therefore to reclaim his old acquaintance, whose good morals and principles he had still a favourable opinion of, he invited him, without mentioning his purpose, to spend some time with him in his retirement at VITERBO, where he then was; and discoursing him sometimes on polite literature, in which FLAMINIO excelled, and at others on points of theology, he gained upon him so insensibly by his insinuating address, as to make him capable of comprehending the great truths of the Catholic

---

orthodoxy of FLAMINIO beyond dispute by two Italian letters of his, one written in 1542, the other in 1543.—But FLAMINIO, by the confession of PALLAVICINI (to whom the most zealous catholics will give credit) was a favourer of LUTHERANISM in 1545, for he says, " He refused to be secretary to " the delegates at the council of TRENT, through his attach- " ment to those opinions, in condemnation of which he must " then have drawn his pen?"

Pallavicini's History Council of Trent, lib. vi.

What became then of this boasted conversion? which PHILIPS places in 1541, viz. " ten years before his death" (vol. i. p. 300.) though PALLAVICINI wisely postpones it to some years after 1545, and PHILIPS ought to have done the same, to make the least consistency in the story—But still his orthodoxy is not cleared up; for pope PAUL IV. eight years after FLAMINIO's death, in 1559, censured many of his works which he wrote at VITERBO, his *Commentaries on the Psalms,* and *his Poems,* and they were accordingly inscribed in the *Catalogue of prohibited books.*

belief;

belief; in which he continued the remainder of his life, and wrote many elegant pieces on sacred subjects, and died at last in the cardinal's family; who used often to say, he looked upon himself as having been serviceable not only to FLAMINIO, but to the whole Catholic cause, by preventing him from revolting to the heretics, to whose party he was strongly inclined, and to whom he would have been a very powerful associate, being master of a pleasing and persuasive style both in his own language and in the Latin [c].

THE

---

[c] As I am in no danger from the resentment of PAUL IV. or his successors, by reading a poem under their censure, and have also the authority of a very admired catholic Mr. POPE, who dared to publish many of them, I will venture to transcribe some elegant *hendecasyllables* of FLAMINIO's writing, during his leisure at VITERBO, which seem to breathe the ease and indolence of that agreeable solitude which inspired them.

CATELLA ad REGINALDUM POLUM.

Cur me, Pole, tuâ venire ad urbem
Lecticâ prohibes? tuæ quid (oro)
Summæ participem benignitatis
Esse non pateris? Canes bonorum
Heroum comites fuêre semper:
Et cœlum canis incolit supremum
Inter sidera: nec polus beata
Sedes cœlicolûm suam catellam
Dedignatur habere secum; at ipsa
Sum despecta tibi, nec unum apud te   10
Angulum valeo impetrare; verùm
Si nostram vacet æstimare formam,

Non

The fortitude of POLE's mind was such as, I dare pronounce, was never equalled by any one of

> Non indigna tuo favore credar.
> Est Pilus mihi lucidus, venustæ
> Pendent auriculæ, nigris ocellis,
> Et caudæ placeo jubis comatæ!
> Nec sum corpore vasta, nec figurâ
> Tam brevi, ut videar puellularum
> Comes dignior esse, quam virorum.
> Nec turpi scabie laboro, nec sunt 20
> Invisi pulices mihi molesti.
> Nec sum prorsus inutilis futura,
> Si lassam recreas, vehisque tecum;
> Nam pedes tibi suaviter fovebo,
> Qui jam frigoribus rigent acutis.
> Nec vero timeas, luto refertâ
> Quod viâ assiduè ambularim, amicus
> Et cliens tuus optimus, MORILLA *
> Me suis manibus piè ac benignè
> Puro flumine terque quaterque lavit; 30
> Et mundâ dedit esse mundiorem
> Sponsâ, quam bona mater ad maritum
> Vult deducere nuptiis paratis.
> Quod si non satis hæc videntur esse
> Ad flectendum animum tuum, catelli,
> Ah! nimis miseri mei catelli
> Te precor moveant; tenella plene
> Quos gestans utero pedes movere
> Vix queo amplius; & tamen necesse est
> Milliaria singulis diebus

* MORILLA was a Spanish gentleman of POLE's family, whom he sent to the cardinals, his colleagues, at TRENT, to deliver his opinion *vivâ voce* on the article of *Justification*.

Multa

our times; it was neither the courage of a philosopher nor of a soldier, but was founded in God, in whom he had so resigned a faith, that he held it an incontestible truth, that whatever HE did, or permitted to be done, was certainly the best; and that it became us not to regret it as an evil, because it appeared so to us, but to be thankful for it, and bear it with patience, if so be it was not brought upon us by any actual demerits of our own. On this principle it was, that he bore up with intrepidity under calumny, banishment, persecution, the loss of friends and dearest relations: I was with him when he received advice of his mother's death, which was attended with the following circumstances. Letters [a] coming in from FRANCE, SPAIN, and

---

Multa conficiam misella, ni te
Volo linquere: sed priùs vel istis
Optem filiolis meis sepulcrum
Fiant viscera matris, ipsa præda
Optarim priùs esse vel luporum,
Quam te, maxime POLE, derelinquam.
Ode M. A. Flaminii—Poemata Italorum, vol. ii.

[a] Neither BECCATELLI, DUDITHIUS, nor GRATIANI, in their enumeration of POLE's characteristic excellencies, choose to mention *his skill in negotiation, or dexterity in the management of business*, but have left them to be recorded among T. PHILLIPS's late *discoveries*. They delight to dwell on his domestic virtues, his studies, and his retirements. They tell you (and the compliment seems to convey a sneer on his public character) that CHARLES V. thought him *il miglior Prete in tutto Christianismo*.

and FLANDERS, he called me to him, as his custom was, to read them over with him, and determine upon proper answers to the several dispatches; when I had examined them, and resolved upon the answers, and was gathering them up in my hand, I observed one of them was written in ENGLISH, upon which I said, "I have no answer ready for "this, for I don't understand the contents of it." To which he replied with great composure, "I "wish you did, that you might see the good news "it contains;" imagining it was really so, "Be "so good, Sir," said I, "to communicate it to "me." He answered, "Till this day I thought "myself highly favoured of God, as being de- "scended from one of the best and noblest women "in ENGLAND, and I valued myself, and was very "grateful to the Divine Goodness for this blessing; "but it has now pleased the Almighty to honour "me still more, and increase my obligation, since "he has now made me *the son of a martyr*, whom "the king of ENGLAND hath brought to the "scaffold, altho' she was seventy years old, and "his own near a relation, for her perseverance in

---

tianismo. But neither the emperor, nor the biographers, give him praise as a *negotiator*; had his last panegyrist been contented to have copied them, in casting that part of his character into shades, he would have given a truer, if not so flattering a picture of him.

a T. PHILLIPS not only asserts in his own name many things contrary to the truth of history, but even introduces his

favourite

" the Catholic faith: in this manner he rewarded
" her for her painful attendance on his daughter;
" but God's will be done." I was thunder-ftruck
at this relation; but he comforted me, saying,
" Let us rejoice rather, for we have now one ad-
" vocate more in heaven." He then turned from
me, and retired to his clofet, where he ftaid about
an hour, and then came out as chearful as before.

This [a] behaviour was not owing to any want of affection for his mother, of whom he always fpake with

---

favourite character POLE as uttering a falfehood, which he really never fpake; in tranflating this paffage from BECCATELLI, he makes the cardinal fay (fpeaking of the COUNTESS OF SALISBURY his mother) " That the king had caufed
" her to be beheaded, though, after his own children, fhe was
" the NEAREST TO HIM IN BLOOD." Whereas BECCATELLI'S words are, *a lui zia*, HIS AUNT, or in true propriety of fpeech, " the firft coufin (not the fifter) of his mother."

Mr. RIDLEY (*the ingenious Reviewer of Phillips's hiftory*) has juftly reproached POLE for fuch an affertion, as he might fairly prefume it to be his; but T. P. will be often found mifinterpreting the words both of friend and foe, fometimes thro' *careleffnefs*, at others thro' *excefs of care*.

[b] BECCATELLI feems to be aware, that this ftoical-apathy of POLE's, in the midft of fo many trying afflictions, may by fome be deemed rather an imputation upon his feelings than a compliment to his fortitude. All who know POLE's ftory, and are converfant in his writings, know, that he had a mind neither above the fenfe of injuries, nor the returns of refentment; but his PEN was his SWORD, and they, againft whom he
drew

with the greatest tenderness, and she herself had an uncommon fondness for him above what she bore to the rest of her children; but the truth was, God had endued him with so extraordinary a portion of his grace, that these misfortunes never could touch him; and afterwards when the *masses* were said for her, he ordered the mass for the Holy Trinity to take place first, and afterwards that *pro defunctis*, according to the order of the Romish church. With the same firmness of mind he received the account of his elder brother HENRY LORD MONTAGUE's death, who was the chief stay of his family, and also of two other near relations of high quality, who suffered with him; and of many other distressful calamities at the same time, which to bear, as he did, one would have almost suspected he had a heart of adamant.

WITH so much candor and simplicity, he had that mixture of prudence and discernment, as to be able to foresee [e] many events, which he was ever dexterous

---

drew it, always found it a very smart and vindictive weapon: whoever shall read his book OF THE UNITY OF THE CHURCH will find THIS CHRISTIAN HERO had as strong feelings of indignation, as the authors either of the *Grecian* or *Roman Philippic*.

[e] The sudden alarm, which seized the imagination of REGINALD upon the execution of the bishop of ROCHESTER, was rather

dexterous to prevent, if they had an alarming appearance: as in the case of the imprisonment of the bishop of ROCHESTER and Sir THOMAS MORE, he concluded, that if the king of ENGLAND was so little scrupulous as to imbrue his hands in the blood of men of that eminence, he would soon become the general executioner of his people; he therefore dispatched a gentleman of his houshold from PADUA, where he then was, to the emperor, to warn him of the danger which threatened his aunt Q. CATHERINE and the whole island, that he might interpose his authority to prevent it.

HE gave another proof of his great judgment, as well as of his attachment to his native country (in whose cause he was never weary of exerting himself) by sending another gentleman of his family in-

---

rather the result of personal apprehension, than of prophetic foresight. The fall of this prelate (tho' the blow was severe) was the great stroke that crushed every rising opposition to the *regal supremacy*, and confirmed that original birth-right of the British monarchy. R. POLE was projecting, if not much advanced in his work, which was to prove the illegality and unwarrantableness of this claim of HENRY's, at the time when FISHER suffered: he began also to look with ambition toward the court of ROME, and to fix his expectations upon those honours which had just been treated with indignity in the person of that BISHOP; who had probably been pardoned in *that* character, if PAUL III. had not indiscreetly added to it, that of CARDINAL OF ST. VITALE.

CARDINAL REGINALD POLE.   159

to FRANCE upon the news of [d] HENRY VIII's death, to procure, if possible, a safe-conduct into ENGLAND to the council of the young king, that he might bring him back to an union with the church, and be the instrument of saving both king

---

[d] Within a twelvemonth of each other died the *two most* dreaded adversaries of the papal power, MARTIN LUTHER and HENRY VIII. The first of which had exposed such a flaw in one of the most costly jewels of the triple crown, THE TREASURE OF INDULGENCIES, as had greatly sunk the boasted value of the whole; and the latter had plucked a second pearl away, *richer than all his tribe,* " The supremacy of an opulent " kingdom."

FATHER PAUL relates with what exceeding joy the news of these two events was received by the council of TRENT, which was then sitting.—First, upon LUTHER's death:

Morì anco à diciotto di Febbraro MARTINO LUTHERO, le quali cose ricevute in TRENTO & a ROMA, non fu sentito tanto dispiacere della mutatione della religione nel palatinato, quanto allegrezza perche fosse morto LUTHERO. (Istoria del Concilio di Trento, Lib. 1.)

And afterwrds, upon the death of HENRY VIII.

Andò aviso della morte del RE d' INGHILTERRA, di che i padri resero grazie a Dio,—attribuendo anco a miracolo che fosse passato di questa vita. (Lib. 1.)

This illustrious assembly of divines! valued not the apostacy of a whole kingdom, in comparison of the death of LUTHER; and returned thanks to God, as for a miracle vouchsafed in their favour, upon the *natural* death of HENRY VIII.

and

and kingdom, by rescuing him from the danger of insurrections among his own subjects, and the invasions with which he might be attacked on the side of FRANCE, FLANDERS, and SCOTLAND. The person he employed on this errand [e] was DR. RICHARD HILLIARD, of an ENGLISH family, and *Penitentiary* of ST. PETER's at ROME; but the deluded kingdom would not pay him the least attention.

NOTWITHSTANDING the singular modesty and mildness of POLE's deportment, he had a certain gravity of manners which, tho' not forbidding, yet procured him reverence, not only from the cardinals, but even from the popes themselves, who were cautious not to say any thing the least unguarded in his presence.

His natural disposition inclined him more to study and contemplation, than to an active life,

---

[e] The letter here mentioned, which POLE sent to the privy council of EDWARD VI. is published by C. QUIRINI, vol. iv. p. 42. and is chiefly relative to his own sufferings in the late reign. It is not very probable the council should pay much attention to such a correspondent, who was known to be employed at the same time in penning inflammatory addresses to the emperor, to spirit him on to interfere in the model of the English government, which CHARLES had shewn a forward inclination to, by some very harsh behaviour to the English ambassador at his court. (QUIRINI, vol. iv. ep. 24.)

which led him, when a young man, to avoid courts and company, and confine himself to books; and even after he became a cardinal, he was never so much himself, as in the solitudes of a monastery.

In his youth he applied himself to *languages*, with uncommon success; in his riper years, when he attached himself to more laborious studies, philosophy and theology [a], he grew indeed somewhat

---

[a] T. Phillips (who translates Dudithius thro' the whole last section of his *Life of Pole*) relates from him a quotation from Cardinal H. Seripandi's Commentaries on St. Paul's Epistles, where he mentions a reply of Pole's to some one who questioned him upon what he thought the most judicious method of studying the abstruse parts of those epistles with success.

"That the most ready way he could propose, was, for the reader to begin at the latter part of the Epistles, where the apostle treats of morality, and to practise what was delivered there; and then go back to the beginning, where the doctrinal parts are reasoned on with great acuteness and subtilty." Phillips's translation of Seripandi, vol. ii. p. 223.

The good and pious reformer J. Wickliff (whom the uncharitable voice of the papal consistory has pronounced *virum damnatæ memoriæ*) was the author of those sentiments 150 years before, and it was his motive for endeavouring to put the scriptures into the hands of the common people in their own language.

"A good

what less curious of his style, yet he still retained that happy talent for composition, which he had acquired by early habit, and which is very evident in the works he hath left behind him: the style of them is rather diffuse, and hath more of the *Asiatic* exuberancy, than of the *Attic* [b] precision, which was owing to that flow of ideas which his luxuriant fancy supplied him with.

He was close in his attention to what he read, and his memory was uncommonly retentive; he had a perfect knowlege of history, both ancient and modern; in philosophy he preferred PLATO to ARISTOTLE, but he soon began to slight these studies, and, devoting himself intirely to the reading of the *scriptures*, dropped all others, and rested

---

" A good life (said he) is the best guide to the knowledge of the scriptures, and he, that keepeth righteousness, hath the true understanding of the Holy Writ." (GILPIN's Life of WICKLIFF.)

[b] C. POLE seems to have *written too much* to be able at all times to *write well*; an indigested profusion of matter has so overloaded many of his epistolary writings, of the latter period of his life, that they are extremely languid and tedious: he seems so much to have accustomed himself to his pen, as not to care to lay it down; and is so elaborately verbose on every occasion of vindicating his conduct, or explaining his plan, that he often leaves the one in suspicion and the other in confusion. (See Quirini, vol. iv. let. 50, 51.)

solely

solely [c] in them: he had formerly been conversant in the Greek and Latin *Fathers* and *Commentators*; but he confined himself latterly to the original text, and became so perfect a master both of the *Old* and *New Testament*, that he seemed to have read nothing else: his constant meditation upon them was surprising, insomuch that I have heard it declared by some of the most learned theologists of our times, "that they never knew an abler master of the "scriptures than Cardinal Pole;" which his writings sufficiently evince.

His custom was, when he was reading any part of the *Holy Writings*, to set down his own thoughts on the subject before him, and compare them afterwards with the opinions of other expositors, and thus, with the joint assistance of both, investigate the sense of the passage.

He has left many curious *tracts* behind him; among which are:

---

[c] Archbishop Parker remarks, "That his predecessor "Pole took this turn, of applying himself solely to the study "of the *scriptures*, during his abode at Viterbo, the natural "result of which studies was, his deviation from his former im- "plicit faith in pontifical decretals and traditions, and his attach- "ment to Lutheranism;" and concludes with saying, *Utinam hoc suscepisset ocyus!* Antiq. Eccl. Brit. p. 519.

The *five* [d] books *on the Unity and Primacy of the church*, addressed to HENRY VIII.

A BOOK

---

[d] BECCATELLI who was very early acquainted with this *notable* work, and knew it under all its forms, has done it the honour of his notice *twice* in the course of this history; he knew it in reality before it had any form at all, when it was sent, sheet by sheet, thro' PRIULI's hands, to CONTARINI, the beginning of 1536, even before the king of England himself was gratified with this eminent *Philippic*.

The first mention Beccatelli makes of it, he speaks of it in these words,

" QUEL LIBRO, c' oggi si vede in stampa." " *The Book*, " which is now printed." In the passage now before us, he calls them,

" *Quei* CINQUE *libri ad Henrico* VIII." " The 5 books " addressed to Henry VIII."

DUDITHIUS, to make up the number of 5 books (as the treatise *De Unitate*, &c. was never divided into more than 4) supposes *the Epistle to Edward* VI. to be the 5*th*, as it was intended by way of *preface* to that work, when POLE did, or designed perhaps only to send it to that young king. But DUDITHIUS is probably mistaken; since it appears from C. QUIRINI's very careful examination, that the epistle to EDWARD VI. was never printed before any edition of the treatise *De Unitate*, &c. nor ever published at all, till within these few years by G. SCHELHORNE. I should therefore suppose it to be a mistake of BECCATELLI's, who might write 5 instead of 4, or he might mean any other of the *apologies*, which POLE occasionally wrote to send, as *prefaces*, with that favourite work; either the APOLOGIA AD CÆSAREM, AD JACOBUM, OR AD

PARLIA-

A book on *General Councils* [a].

Two books, ON THE DUTIES OF THE PAPAL OFFICE, written in the form of *dialogue* between the Cardinal D'Urbino and himself, in the [b] conclave,

---

PARLIAMENTUM ANGLIÆ (all which HENRY VIII. might possibly have seen) rather than that written to EDWARD VI. which was not drawn up till after his death, and could never possibly have been addressed or sent to him.

[a] This book *De Concilio* (which T. PHILLIPS tells his readers in one part of his works was published by ALDUS MANUTIUS, and addressed to PAUL IV. and in another by PAULUS MANUTIUS, and dedicated to PIUS IV.) was printed in 1562, the year before DUDITHIUS gave his Translation of POLE's Life from the MS. in Italian by BECCATELLI.

POLE wrote the above treatise during the month he staid behind his colleagues the cardinals DI MONTE and SANTA CROCE at ROME, who urged him to follow them to *Trent* where there was business to be done; but he did not join them till his work was finished, and the roads clear of the supposed assassins from England. This apprehension of his, his friends thought very lightly of (as appears from many passages in VI. of the *Italian* letters published from MARCELLUS's MSS. (Quirini, vol. iv. p. 184.) But, like the poet EUMOLPAS (in PETRONIUS) " He retired into a corner to write a description of the storm, " instead of assisting his comrades in working the ship."

[b] The first sketch of this work was a single DIALOGUE in Italian written in his CELL in the CONCLAVE, and sent with a letter appendant to it to a young cardinal in the same assembly.

clave, during the long contest which preceded the election of Julius III.

A TREATISE, ON THE ^cMETHOD OF PREACHING.

ANOTHER, ON THE ^d REFORMATION OF THE CHURCH OF ENGLAND.

MANY comments and devout meditations on several of the PSALMS, and PROPHETICAL writings;

The letter sent with it is printed in C. Quirini's vol. iv. dated (ex cellâ meâ xiii calend. Feb. 1550.). DUDITHIUS says, he enlarged it afterwards to 5 books.—Such was the restless pen of this indefatigable writer!

^c Cardinal QUIRINI presumes he hath discovered this work of POLE's, which he has given us in his 3d vol. under the title of " Literæ Pontificiæ de Modo Concionandi," p. 75, &c. it having been very usual with PAUL III. in whose name these pontifical letters were published, to make use of C. POLE's pen, as BECCATELLI has observed in the course of this history; and C. QUIRINI's conjecture is strengthened by an Italian letter of POLE's to CONTARINI, signifying his being employed by that pontiff to give his opinion in writing *del modo di predicare*, not long before these *pontifical* letters were set-forth. Quirini, vol. iii. p. 45.

^d This was the title given at ROME to POLE's 12 synodical decrees (proposed to the convocation in the king's chapel at *Westminster*, in Nov. 1555) when they were published in Italy in 1564. (See Archbishop Parker's Antiq. Eccles. Brit. p. 528.

and

CARDINAL REGINALD POLE. 167

and *a large collection of letters*, fraught with sentiments both of genius and piety; all which, I hope, will appear ᵉ to the world in due time.

ᵉ The reputation of perfecting this task, which BECCATELLI so much wished to see, but neither himself nor Cardinal MORONE lived to execute, was reserved for the accomplishment of C. ANGELO MARIA QUIRINI, bishop of BRESCIA, after an interval of almost two centuries: his station of KEEPER OF THE VATICAN LIBRARY enabled him to make a more exact scrutiny after all the literary remains of the English cardinal than fell within the ability of any other person, especially since the archives of that library have been guarded with that jealous eye as they are now reputed to be; to these personal opportunities he added also a very extraordinary zeal to extend his inquiries thro' every quarter where any possible materials might be collected for the enlargement of his design, and searched all the public and private libraries at VENICE, BOLOGNA, FLORENCE, SIENNA, &c. for all the letters that passed between CONTARINI, MARCELLUS, PRIULI, BECCATELLI, and others of POLE's friends and correspondents. From these several storehouses he amassed in his life time sufficient materials for 4 large volumes, which were published at his own press at BRESCIA between the years 1744 and 1752. A FIFTH volume has been added to those (from the collections he had himself made, and deposited in the Brescian library) by the learned CURATORS, in the year 1757, since his decease.

The access I have had to that large and curious collection of POLE's *Remains*, in which the *Italian* tracts have been the principal objects of my attention, I owe to DR. NEVE, *the learned and accurate animadverter upon Mr. Phillips's History of the Life of Cardinal Pole.*

He was very strict and regular in his private devotions, and reserved in conversation with his own family.

Before he was ordained *priest* he received the *communion* every Sunday; and I have been told by the bishop of St. Asaph, who was his chaplain for some years, that when he was abroad in any place of retirement, as at Capranica or the like, he ordered mass to be said, and would assist the priest who officiated, as his *Acolothist*, during the whole service, and help him to robe and disrobe, leaving it only to one of his servants to hold the *napkins*. When he became priest, after his settlement in England, he always said mass himself every Sunday if not oftener.

His virtues were known and admired in all parts of Europe, Charles V. knew him perfectly, and held him in great estimation; but reasons of state, and his attention to the French war, would not suffer him to give those public testimonies of his regard which he was inclined to do, for fear of provoking the king of England to take part against him.

A person of great eminence told me, that as he was talking with the emperor, of the cardinals and the court of Rome, his Imperial majesty said [f],

---

[f] If Mr. Ridley's ingenious hypothesis be the true one (Ridley's Review, p. 20.) this compliment of the emperor's was

CARDINAL REGINALD POLE.   169

"He did not know a better prieſt in Chriſtendom "than the Cardinal of ENGLAND;" and HENRY II. ⁵ of FRANCE, as I have mentioned before, "regretted he was not better acquainted "with POLE's merits upon PAUL III's vacancy, if ſo "he would have had no other pope but POLE."

MANY perſons ſpeak of him to this day as of a character ſurpaſſing human perfection; and I have often heard the Cardinal of TRENT ſay, he valued himſelf principally upon two circumſtances in his life, "That ᵃ he was *ſervant* to CHARLES V. and

---

was the leaſt flattering to Pole's ambition of any he could poſſibly have made him; and from a prince of Charles's avowed diſregard of all churchmen, popes as well as cardinals, it appears to have more of ſarcaſm than civility: T. PHILLIPS, willing to make it ſound better, interprets it differently, and makes the emperor ſay, he did not know a better MAN than the Engliſh cardinal. Vol. ii. p. 239.

ˢ T. PHILLIPS chooſes to aſcribe this compliment to FRANCIS I. inſtead of HENRY II. in which he has had the misfortune to fall into a ſmall *anachroniſm*, as FRANCIS I. died 2 years before PAUL III. and therefore could not eaſily "have given "Pole his intereſt (as PHILLIPS mentions) at the death of that "pope," vol. ii. p. 239.

ᵃ It cannot be ſuppoſed, that FULKE GREVIL, LORD BROOK, ever heard of this ſaying of the cardinal of TRENT; yet it is remarkable how exactly he has copied it, in his own monumental inſcription.

FULKE GREVIL, *Servant* to QUEEN ELIZABETH (*Counſellor* to KING JAMES) and *Friend* to SIR PHILIP SIDNEY.

"*friend*

"*friend* to REGINALD POLE;" whom he used to call *his saint* POLE.

HE had great intimacy with the persons of the first character for parts and learning, in the early season of his life; but after he was made a cardinal his principal connection was with Contarini, Bembo, Morone, and Badia: the illustrious Signora Victoria Colonna, marchioness of PESCARA, a lady of an elevated genius, and distinguished accomplishments, had so great an affection for him, that she bequeathed him a legacy of *ten thousand ducats*, which lay in the *bank* of VENICE. The cardinal would not accept them for himself, but settled them as a portion upon her niece VICTORIA (the daughter of her brother ASCANIO COLONNA) who was married afterwards to DON GARCIA OF TOLEDO. This was an effort of generosity greatly to the cardinal's honour, which few perhaps may choose to imitate; but he had a spirit which raised him above every interested consideration.

SUCH were the studies [b], the atchievements, and manners, of this extraordinary person, which I have

---

[b] BECCATELLI does not seem to aim at presenting us with a complete CATALOGUE of POLE's works, in the short list he hath given us, but is satisfied with enumerating the principal ones, which were either printed under his name, or well known to

have collected into one view in this short history, rather for the instruction and imitation of myself and

---

to be of his composing, at the time he drew up this PANEGYRIC to his memory.

DUDITHIUS, who published his *Latin* paraphrase in 1563, *five* years after POLE's death, hath made some additions to the *Italian* catalogue, adding to it *His Discourse on Peace*, and some other *tracts* which he wrote after his return to ENGLAND.

Vita Poli, vol. i. sect. 42. Quirini.

T. PHILLIPS hath augmented it still more, though his additions are very partial and imperfect (vol. ii. p. 224.) inserting only those he thinks most to his honour, and omitting others which were the offspring of passion or religious frenzy.

He might otherwise have given us, from the same storehouse where he found the rest (*The Collections of C. Quirini*) a more copious and perfect enumeration of the writings of his admired author: *there* he would have been directed to—

—His cruel and insulting epistle to the *devoted* CRANMER—His *Four* remarkable *Apologies*—fraught with the bitterest invectives against HENRY VIII. both living and dead.

QUIRINI, vol. i. & iv.

—His Letter of *Instruction* to PAUL III.—before he entered on his rebellious embassy against the peace of ENGLAND; wherein he exhorts him to raise a fund for the support of the ENGLISH rebels, and to endeavour to persuade the emperor to make peace with the TURKS, that he may be better able to second him in this enterprise against POLE's native country—

Quirini Monumenta, vol. ii. p. 274.

Many letters to CHARLES V.'s and FRANCIS I.'s ministers on the same project—

Quirini, vol. ii. ep. 17, 54, 55, &c.

and of those who may vouchsafe to read it, than to attempt doing honour to my subject which needs no increase of reputation; and I doubt not but whoever

---

LETTERS TO Q. MARY—to deter her from maintaining her *Supremacy* both in church and state, which she was very unwilling to give up—

Quirini, vol. iv. ep. 43. 46.

OTHER LETTERS—to assure her she had no other sanction that could establish the legitimacy of her birth, but the *Papal Dispensation*—

Tria Poli Scripta, Quirini, vol. v. p. 150, &c.

LETTERS OF CONGRATULATION TO K. PHILIP—on the marvellous felicity brought upon this nation by his condescending to reign over them—

Quirini, vol. iv. ep. 54, 55.

Many extravagant encomiums on that greatest national *blessing*, THE SPANISH MATCH—

Quirini, vol. iv. ep. 51.

Whoever, therefore, upon a fair and impartial examination of POLE's literary remains, will endeavour to make a true and just estimate of his real character, may in one place perhaps be pleased with his taste for composition: in another, with his critical judgment on the labours of others: in a third, with his delicate address to his friends: and in a fourth, some may even admire his spirited attack upon his enemies: but they must ever reproach him for his pusillanimous adulation of those he stood in awe of, and his indecent invectives upon those who had offended him; they must ever detest his cruel mockery of CRANMER, and despise him for his abject flattery of that most odious and despicable character King PHILIP— They must laugh at that frantic piece of most nonsensical enthusiasm which

ever will examine the calamitous events of his story, the persecutions he suffered in his own person, and the share he bore in the misfortunes of his friends and his family, will think him worthy to be enrolled among the order of MARTYRS [c].

---

which he wrote to the Spanish bishop NAVARRA, however they may admire the ingenious letter to J. SADOLET.

In fine, there is that *alloy* in the character both of the writer and the man, which no *refinement* of the PANEGYRIST can ever separate; so that although one should applaud the POLITE STUDENT, the RELIGIOUS RECLUSE, and the BENEVOLENT PATRON AND FRIEND: one must ever censure the INSOLENT APOLOGIST, the SEDITIOUS NEGOTIATOR, the TIMID MINISTER, and the BIGOTTED LEGATE.

[c]. BECCATELLI, having thus attended his hero to his tomb, and pronounced this pompous ELOGY over him, is not satisfied with the honours he has paid to his memory, but is so zealous for his *Canonization*, that he is guilty of a great breach of *historical justice* to prove his qualification; since he seems to have so little plea for the *Crown of Martyrdom*, that there is scarce an example to be found in any period of our annals, of one whose final *catastrophe* was so perfectly easy and undisturbed as REGINALD POLE's.

APPENDIX

APPENDIX.

*———moveat cornicula risum
Furtivis nudata coloribus———* HORAT.

THE *Compiler* of the late HISTORY OF THE LIFE OF REGINALD POLE, was pleased to value himself exceedingly upon the novelty and ORIGINALITY of a former performance of his, *A Letter on the Study of Divinity*, and has complimented himself thereupon in an uncommon strain of vanity and self-applause.

"It may perhaps (he says,) be a weakness to confess, that the novelty of the subject has conduced not a little to make me go thro' the performance with alacrity: for tho' there may be, for any thing I know, several methods, treatises, and essays on the study of DIVINITY; it is a testimony I owe to truth, when I tell you I never saw one that "has

" has any affinity with this: and the produc-
" tion, as well as the conduct of the piece be-
" ing my own, it has been *wrote* from per-
" suasion and sentiment; and, I hope, with a
" view to recommend, not myself, but the
" subject." As he has no pretence to boast of any such exclusive right and property in his *late* work, which is very little more than *a compilation* from the larger work of CARDINAL QUIRINI, the same *testimony he owes to truth*, should induce him to make the acknowledgment; which he probably could not do better than in the following *parody* of his own *inimitable* paragraph.

" It may perhaps be a weakness in me to
" confess that *the novelty of Cardinal Quirini's
" work* has conduced not a little to make me
" go thro' THIS performance with alacrity: for
" tho' there may be, for any thing I know,
" several other authors, historians, divines, and
" biographers, who have written on this sub-
" ject; it is a testimony I owe to truth, when
" I tell you, *I translated chiefly from him*, and
" scarce ever saw one of them. The produc-
" tion therefore and the conduct of the piece
" being *none of my own*, it has been wrote from
" persuasion and sentiment, that all the Cardinal
" *advanced*

"*advanced must be true*, and, I hope, with a view to recommend *both* myself and my subject."

[See Letter on the Study of Divinity, by T. P. p. 113].

That the reader may agree with him, and applaud the justness of this confession; he will please to attend him, step by step, with the Cardinal at his side, from whom he seldom ventures to stray, unless some other GUIDE takes him by the hand, and leads him forward.

It may be requisite to inform the reader, who is unacquainted with C. QUIRINI's work, that he has followed the plan of Dr. MIDDLETON with respect to CICERO, and extracts MINUTES of REGINALD POLE's life from the substance of his epistolary correspondence, and other tracts of his, which were ample enough to supply him with materials for a competent history of him, with the addition of the elegant panegyric written by BECCATELLI.

These memoirs the Cardinal has broken into several distinct chapters, and given the progress of R. POLE's Life, in a chronological method.

178   APPENDIX.

The firſt chapter of this DIATRIBA or Diſſertation, comprehends the five firſt years of POLE's life and academical education at PADUA, after he had left the Engliſh univerſity, at about twenty years of age, till his return to England in 1525.

How luckily this coincides with T. PHILLIPS's plan, will be very obvious to the reader, and he may be curious to know the uſe he has made of it, tho' Mr. P. himſelf would have kept it a ſecret.

N. B. The few firſt pages which reſpect POLE's OXFORD education, before C. QUIRINI takes him up, are taken from A. WOOD's ATHæ. OXONs.

PLA-

PLAGIARISMS

FROM

CARDINAL QUIRINI

APPENDIX.

T. P.		
22 p. note.	Extract from LONGOLIUS's letter to SAULIUS.	QUIRINI, 209.
23	GIBERTI's character,	QUIRINI, 268.
24 n.	BEMBO's letter to POLE, for which he refers to the VENICE edition of his epistles,	QUIRINI, ep. 5.
24 n.	PHILLIPS, in opposition to BECCATELLI and DUDITHIUS, hath (out of the regard he professes to accuracy even in things immaterial) prolong'd POLE's stay at PADUA, or rather sent him back to spend another year there; because a letter of ERASMUS to him, and two of BEMBO's are dated in 1526; whereas QUIRINI more modestly supposes, ERASMUS might not know POLE had left PADUA when he wrote his letter; and BEMBO's letters he is convinced are falsly dated, QUIRINI, 217 & 270. PHILLIPS had therefore better have acquiesced with QUIRINI, in what POLE's biographers relate, than have bent his history to a compliance with the dates of three suspected letters.	
31 and 32	The two quotations from ERASMUS, on the flourishing state of literature in the court of ENGLAND, tho' referred to the BASIL edition of ERASMUS, are from QUIRINI, p. 221 & 232.	

QUIRINI's Diatriba, cap. 2. vol. 1.
PHILLIPS Sect. 1. p. 33, &c.

33 and 34	From BECCATELLI's Life of POLE,	vol. 5. QUIRINI.
42 to 46	Translated from POLE's APOLOGIA AD CÆSAREM,	QUIRINI, vol. 1.
46 and 47	Account of Dean COLET, and the quotation from ERASMUS, where he makes the ridiculous blunder (noted by Dr. NEVE) of calling JONAS ERFORDIENSIS,	

APPENDIX.

T. P.	
	FORDIENSIS, BISHOP of HEREFORD, and writes page 435, instead of ep. 435, all from QUIRINI, Diat. cap. 2. p. 231.
60 n.	His quotation from LARRE'E, HIST. D' ANGLETERRE, except that he mistook in the reference, 295 for 259, from QUIRINI, p. 240.
61	The long quotation from POLE's book De UNITATE, he found to his hand in QUIRINI, p. 234, as also that remarkable passage in the note (p. 62.) which seems to contain a sarcasm of POLE's not founded in history; and again that apostrophe to the spirit of HENRY VII. QUIRINI, p. 237, 238.

QUIRINI's Diatriba, c. 3.
PHILLIPS, Sect. 1. p. 64, &c.

64	The interview with the King, from BECCATELLI, and the letter to EDWARD VI. 4th & 5th C. QUIRINI.
71, 72 note.	The chastisement so liberally bestowed on Bishop BURNET is not his own, but QUIRINI's, p. 242. and also the learned strictures upon RAPIN, LARRE'E, BOSSUET, NICERON, and LE GRAND, are all in QUIRINI, p. 249.
73	The long Story of Lord CROMWELL's endeavouring to instil MACHIAVEL's politicks into HENRY, and of POLE's being the first detector of the mischievous tendency of MACHIAVEL's writings, are pointed out by QUIRINI, p. 263. who directed him to the APOLOGIA AD CÆSAREM in vol. 1. from which he has very liberally translated six or seven pages.
80	PHILLIPS has followed QUIRINI so methodically, as to close his first section with the last quota-

tion

APPENDIX.

T. P.

80   tion he found in QUIRINI's third chapter, the letter from ERASMUS; part of which he gives in his note to p. 80.   QUIRINI, 268.

QUIRINI's Diatriba, cap. 4.
PHILLIPS, Sect. 2.

81   How does PHILLIPS know that LAURA's tomb was discovered on POLE's arrival? Why QUIRINI tells him, CASTELLANUS a friend of BEMBO's and Dean of AVIGNON, had lately received two letters from him, one of which congratulated him, on PERUSINUS's discovery of LAURA's tomb. PHILLIPS therefore fixes it at a venture to the precise time of POLE's arrival, and quotes his reference from BEMBI ep. lib. 6. p. 279, instead of QUIRINI, cap. 4. p. 274.

82   A translation from QUIRINI, p. 279. with this mistake, that ALCIATE according to QUIRINI, *commigravit Biturigas* which is Latin for BOURGES, and not BEZIERS as P. construes it.

83 to 98   His intimacy and correspondence with SADOLET, and the several letters between GIBERTI, BONAMICO, BEMBO, &c. with the contest between POLE and SADOLET upon the proper object of their studies, in consequence of POLE's visit to Carpentras, is an uniform translation of QUIRINI, cap. 4. from p. 274. to 288, except that P. has lengthened the subject by enlarging his quotations from the several letters there referred to.

98   Account of BUNET (properly BUNEL) with PAULUS MANUTIUS's testimony of his merits.
                            QUIRINI, 288.

APPENDIX.

T. P.
98 to 102 — The characters of POLE's learned friends, CONTARINI, BEMBO, CARAFFA, PRIULI, BECCATELLI, &c. he has faithfully translated, without one grateful acknowledgment, from QUIRINI's Diatriba, cap. 4. and part of the 5th.

QUIRINI, cap. 5.
PHILLIPS, Sect. 2. p. 103.

99 & 100 — The reference to ERASMUS's epistle in the margin, and the quotation from BEMBO's Italian letter in the note, are both to be found in QUIRINI, 295 & 299.

112 & 113 — The first opening of his account of POLE's work *de Unitate*, &c. and also of SAMPSON's and GARDINER's treatises, QUIRINI, 308 & seq.

120 & seq. — After making large extracts thro' several pages from the apology to CHARLES V. in QUIRINI, vol. 1. he returns to his DIATRIBA and translates 310, 311. and following pages. The remaining pages to p. 131. are scraps from POLE's letters on the subject of his book DE UNITATE, or extracts from the APOLOGY to CHARLES V. all to be found in QUIRINI's DIATRIBA, c. 5.

131 n. — The congregated blunders in this note upon VERGER, have been fully exposed by Dr. NEVE. The remark upon VERGER is QUIRINI's, the mistakes PHILLIPS's, p. 325.

133 — The account of the PREFACE addressed to JAMES V. King of Scotland, taken from QUIRINI, vol. 1. Prefatio ad Monim². Prælim. p. 96. not referred to.

APPENDIX.

T. P.	
134 n.	The quotation from BURNET, QUIRINI, p. 329.
	The MUTILATED quotation from VERGER (for which difingenuous artifice he has been deservedly reprimanded by Dr. NEVE,) is *at full length in*, QUIRINI, p. 374.
134 & 135	QUIRINI, 348 & feq.
136 n.	P. MANUTIUS's letter to SAULIUS, lib. 1. QUIRINI, 349.
137, &c.	QUIRINI, 350 & feq.

QUIRINI, caput ultimum Diatribæ.
PHILLIPS, Section 2. p. 138.

138	QUIRINI, 364—65.
139 & 140 n.	The history of the *Riforma*, and the very learned note, fuggefting a reafon why the PLAN was inferted by A. BLADI 1538, and not by SURIUS in his collection, is literally from QUIRINI, p. 367.

QUIRINI, vol. 2. Diatriba ad Epiftolas.
PHILLIPS, Section 3.

151	The compliment to PAUL III. on his choice of Cardinals, QUIRINI, p. xxix.
155	The account of S. HOSIUS, and his remark on ERASMUS, and also the note underneath, QUIRINI, p. xliv.
189 to 203	The Relation of POLE's firft embaffy 1537, is taken from BECCATELLI's hiftory, and the fubftance of five or fix letters from POLE to CONTARINI, which are paraphrafed in QUIRINI's Diatriba ad Epiftolas, Sectio 2.

APPENDIX. 185

T. P.	
204 205	The account how POLE and his friends spent their time at LIEGE, falsly referred to Monim^a. Prelim^{ia}. whereas the whole is tranflated from fome extracts from PRIULI's Italian letters quoted by QUIRINI, Diatriba, p. civ. &c.
206	The anecdote from COCKLEY, which he pretends in the note, to quote, 'A COMMENT^{IS}. DE ACTIS LUTHERI; he undoubtedly took from the next page in QUIRINI, where the fame reference is precifely to be found, QUIRINI, p. cvi.
210	ERASMUS's teftimony to the liberality of ERARD LA MARC, which he pretends to take from ERASMUS's works, he tranfcribed from QUIRINI, p. ciii.

QUIRINI, Diatriba ad Epift. vol. 2.
PHILLIPS, Sect, 4. vol. 1.

232 note.	A long vindication of PIGHIUS, and the account of his work, with the note to page 232, is to be found, QUIRINI, p. cxxx.
234 n.	The anecdotes concerning CAMILLUS URSINI, and the reference to his life, printed at VENICE 1566, QUIRINI, Diat. p. clxi. & ii.
236 n.	His obfervations on the interview at NICE, and his pompous reference to ten different authors are all to be found QUIRINI, Diat. Sect. viii.
241	His relation how POLE and his friends paffed their time at PRIULI's villa, with all their names, and the quotation from BEMBO's letter to BRUNO in the notes, QUIRINI, p. clxxxv.

237 The

T. P.	
237	The Pope's right of excommunication vindicated, QUIRINI, p. clv.
243	The progress of POLE's second embassy, QUIRINI, Diatribæ Sect. ix.
246 & seq.	His remarks on the execution of POLE's relations, QUIRINI, p. cc.
249	The quotation from SADOLET's LETTERS, to which he refers in the note, from QUIRINI, p. cxcvii.
259 note.	His digression to the Diet at FRANCFORT, and his learned references to ANNALES RAYNALDI, and PALLAVICINI, from QUIRINI, Diatrib. p. ccxvi.
262	The account of SADOLET's work DE ÆDIFICATIONE ECCLESIÆ, tho' he quotes QUIRINI's reference, and not himself, is to be found QUIRINI, p. cciv. & seq.
263	His very sage criticism upon DU PIN's and NICERON's omission of this work of SADOLET's, and MONTFAUCON's mention of it among the VATICAN MSS. is unhappily forestalled by QUIRINI, p. ccxiii.
269	His long quotation from J. SADOLET's letter to Cardinal FARNESE is quoted *totidem verbis*, by QUIRINI, ccxiii.
271	PHILLIPS is so blind a copier of QUIRINI, that he inserts the remarkable fit of enthusiasm which seized POLE in the grotto of ST. BEAUME, in the wrong place, as QUIRINI confesses *he* has done (vol. 2. p. ccxlv.) but he was not prosecuting a regular series of history; PHILLIPS (if he was determined to tell so absurd a tale) should have placed it on POLE's journey back from TOLEDO to AVIGNON in MARCH (page 253) when

APPENDIX.

T. P.
271   when he passed near St. Beaume; not on his route from Carpentras to Verona in October, when he never went near it.

277   He here follows Quirini, in placing the account of Bembo and the letters which passed between him and Pole, on Bembo's promotion, out of their place. Quirini did it, not to disturb the series of letters he was giving an account of, but P. as a biographer should have related facts in their chronological order.

> Quirini, vol. 3.
> Phillips, Sect. 5.

286   The account of Contarini's treatise De Justificatione and the difference of the Paris edition of 1571. from the Venetian of 1589.
> Quirini, vol. iii. p. ccxii. where they are collated.

286   The opinion of Sadolet on *predestination*; the note underneath from his letters; and the concluding stroke of genius, "That as the "Errors of Jansenius," &c. are the sentiments and words of Quirini, p. 86 de Viterb. Sodal. Vol. 3. "Jansenisticæ "doctrinæ tumulum in Sadoletica reperiri "quorundam doctorum effatum est; pari rati-"one insignem cladem a Contarino & Po-"lo retulisse doctrinam Lutheranam di-"cendum erit."

Quirini,

QUIRINI, vol. iiii. Apparatus ad Epistolas.
PHILLIPS, Section vi. vol. i.

T. P.	
332	SADOLET's letter to POLE which he quotes as from Lugd. edit. 1560. He found in QUIRINI, v. iii. ep. 4.
335	POLE's letter to the POPE on the abrupt dissolution of the first council at TRENT is given by QUIRINI on the same occasion. App. ad vol. 4. p. xi.
336	The account of GIBERTI's legacies to POLE from BECCATELLI's life, which he takes no notice of. QUIRINI, vol. 5.
336 n.	The several references to ERASMUS, and SADOLET. QUIRINI.
358 & seq.	The compliment to POLE on his two letters to COCKLEY, is litterally taken from QUIRINI. App. ad ep. p. xiii.
362 to 366	Proceeds regularly with a translation from QUIRINI's apparatus vol. 4. from p. xvii. to xxi. with only the trouble of referring to the letters in the notes, and transferring QUIRINI's comment on them into his text.

QUIRINI, vol. iv.
PHILLIPS, section 7.

436 & seq.	He resumes the plan of QUIRINI's APPARATUS, and gives the same extracts from the letters, only enlarging them to increase the bulk of his work. App. vol. 4. p. xxii. & seq.

T. P.	
441	His account of the letter to EDWARD VI. and the learned note at the bottom, translated from QUIRINI, p. xxxiv. App.
451 to 458	The whole history of the proceedings in the conclave wherein POLE was set aside, and C. DI MONTE elected, he copied from BECCATELLI, or his PARAPHRAST; tho' his flourishes on POLE's disinterested conduct He found in QUIRINI, p. xxxviii. App.
460 last p. vol. 1.	POLE's motive, tho' the wrong one, for retiring to MAGUZANO, copied *verbatim* from QUIRINI, which I shall place at length before the reader, that he may from hence form his judgment of the rest, and observe how liberally Mr. P. borrows, what he has not the gratitude to acknowledge.

PHILLIPS's last p. vol. 1.

Being now in the 53d year of his age, he was desirous to pass the evening of his life in privacy. He had an additional inducement, the loss of those who were accustomed to share the weight of business with him; the cardinals CONTARINI, BEMBO, SADOLET, CORTESIUS, and BADIA, and GIBERTI bishop of VERONA were dead, &c.

QUIRINI, apparatus vol. iv. p· xlvi.

Anno liii. rerum humanarum quodammodo tædio affectus, et præsertim ex obitu eorum quibuscum magna ipsi familiaritas, et usus intercesserat, nimirum, præter CONTARINUM, BEMBI, SADOLETI, CORTESII, et BADIÆ Cardinalium;

et

APPENDIX.

et præterea GIBERTI episcopi VERONENSIS, VICTORIÆ COLUMNÆ, &c.

QUIRINI, vol. 4 and 5.
PHILLIPS, vol. 2.

p. 6. n. — The letter to the queen of ENGLAND, for which he refers in the note to ODORICUS RAYNALDUS. tom. xxi. ANNAL. ECCLES. he found with the fame reference,

QUIRINI, Addenda vol. 4.

7, &c. — The several letters between MARY and POLE before he left MAGUZANO, and his flow advances towards BRUSSELS in his way to ENGLAND, which are the substance of these pages, are all inserted in QUIRINI's 4th vol. and commented upon in his APPARATUS,

Section ix. x. vol. 4. app.

42 — The ORATIO DE PACE PHILLIPS says, "is a long discourse and written in Italian." He should have said, "was written originally in Italian, as PHOLIUS who translated it into Latin mentions in his dedication to the Cardinal de Medici," but PHILLIPS's ENGLISH version is from PHOLIUS's LATIN,

p. 402, &c. vol. 4. QUIRINI.

75 to 84 — POLE's journey, from his first departure from BRUSSELS to the completion of the legate's triumph over the two states of the nation by bringing them again under the papal yoke, is from an Italian tract published in QUIRINI, vol. v. p. 303, intitled, "Il felicissimo ritorno del regno "d'Inghilterra."

124 C.

APPENDIX.

T. P.	
124 a.	C. POLE's admonition for calling a synod, directed to BONNER bishop of LONDON, for which he quotes Regis. Bonner, et Concil. Mag. Brit. vol. iv. p. 131. is in QUIRINI's appendix to vol. v. p. 227. with the same reference to WILKINS.
211 n.	He quotes POLE's will, as if he had seen it elsewhere, and not in QUIRINI, where it is to be found, vol. v. p. 181. with the reference which PHILLIPS prefer'd. Testamen C. Poli ex cod. MS. bibliothicæ Ambrosianæ.
212 n.	The *supposed* letter to Q. MARY for which he learnedly quotes T. HEARNE, p. 122, from the MS. COLL. OF T. SMYTH, he found with the same reference, QUIRINI, vol. v. p. 275.
214	He says, " POLE died the morning of the 17th December," this he translated unluckily from DUDITHIUS in QUIRINI's first vol. who writes, " 17 KALENDAS DECEMBRIS e vitâ migravit" which he first translates, and then corrects equally wrong in his table of ERRATA, for the 17 Kal. Dec^{ris}. is neither the 17th of DECEMBER, nor the 18th of NOVEMBER.
216	The letter written by PAUL SADOLET to an anonymous person, but supposed by the publishers of QUIRINI's 5th vol. to be designed for PRIULI; PHILLIPS found in the APPENDIX p. 243. vol. v. Quirini, with the reference to COLL. EP. ITAL. BER. PINI. l. 3. which he has adopted to deceive his readers.

PHILLIPS's, section the last.

The whole of this SECTION is a literal translation from the latter part of BECCATELLI's life of POLE,

APPENDIX.

Pole, or perhaps rather from his translator Dudithius, disguised only by a few transpositions, and enlarged with part of two letters from Pole to Miranda, archbishop of Toledo.

FALSE

FALSE TRANSLATIONS,
AND
FALSE REFERENCES, &c.

'Mr. PHILLIPS, it may be supposed, has taken uncommon pains to give a true and elegant version of POLE'S FIRST LETTER UPON RECORD, which he selected from the rest, in order to do honour to POLE's abilities, by presenting the reader with so ingenious a specimen of them; and also to do credit to himself, by exhibiting a perfect and polish'd translation of it, in his own language. As I don't find one expression that bears any relation to the following in POLE'S LATIN letter, the nonsense in the ENGLISH translation, must belong solely to Mr. PHILLIPS.

T. P.
87 p.
vol. 1.

AS the sun never withdraws his rays, but alternately transfers the day to all who stand in need of it, so *in this illustrious course of merit*, the instructions of Sadolet have continued the same.
PHILLIPS's translation of POLE's letter to J. SADOLET. Appendix, No. ii. vol. 2.

85   for September 1552, read September 1525.
91   BUNET's true name, was PIERRE BUNEL.
131 n.   SCHELHORNE, professor at MEMMINGHEN, not HAMBURG.
136   "About *this* time (says P.) CHARLES V. was expected in ITALY to be crown'd by the Pope," viz. 1536.

O   Cardinal

APPENDIX.

T. P.

Cardinal QUIRINI would tell him p. 298. vol. 1. that CHARLES V. went to BOLOGNA for that purpose five years before at least.

150 p. n. False reference; POLE's letter to PAUL III, is in QUIRINI's vol. 2d. not 1st.

153 p. n. False reference; the letter referr'd to is in vol. ii. ep. 1. not ep. ii. vol. 1.

The letter itself PHILLIPS recommends for "*its elegance and good sense in an unusual degree*;" the reader will judge of his translation of it, from the concluding paragraph.

"As the kind and advantageous sentiments we feel IN YOUR REGARD cannot be brought within the compass of a letter, we have ordered our embassador to declare more fully the republic's sentiments and my dispositions IN YOUR RE-GARD." PHILLIPS's TRANSLATION.

154 n. False reference; part 10. should be part 11.

In the letter he has omitted to translate a passage peculiarly characteristic of Pole's disposition,

"ενθουσιασμος ille tuus nos non latet."

176 n. False reference; it is not in page 217, but 267.

193 False reference; not in page 51, but 47.

207 The extract from the POPE's letter to the king of the ROMANS is falsely translated, to do honour to POLE: he does not "intreat his majesty to provide *every thing for his security*, and to write to those princes thro' whose territories he was to pass, to do the same:" PHILLIPS.

But being, as he owns, SOLLICITUS NE QUID CARDINALI NOCEATUR, he requests him, "OPERAM DARE UT SECURE PER GERMANIAM REDIRE POSSIT."

PAULUS iii. REGI ROMAN.

208 False

APPENDIX.

T.P.	
208 n.	False reference; for 48 read 87; again, for 71 read 72.
242 n.	It is not, inter Monimenta Præliminaria.
283 margin	The letter dated 22 April 1541, is not from CAPRANICA but ROME,
	<div align="right">QUIRINI, vol. iii. p. 23.</div>
284	He asserts " that POLE had advised CONTARINI, to reduce all the articles in dispute to the sole question of *justification*." Whereas there is not the shadow for asserting POLE to have been the *adviser* of this, in the letters from which he quotes his authority.
287 margin.	CONTARINI did not die September 1 1542: BECCATELLI, who writes his life, and was with him when he died, says, alli 24 d'AGOSTO su'l mezzo dì rese l'anima a dio.
	Vita del C. Contarini p. 135. vol. iii. Quirini.
307 n.	The letter to the cardinal of MANTUA is not among the ITALIAN letters; it is LATIN.
310	The Italian letters referr'd to, QUIRINI vol. iii. p. 99. say not a word " *of the three Italians being hired by the king.*"
298	BECCATELLI, PARPALIA, and ORMANET, were not " ALL persons of great distinction, " who followed POLE's fortunes from no other " motive than their personal attachment."
	BECCATELLI was his secretary till he was removed to RAGUSA, and PERPALIA, was a poor ABBÉ of SAVOY, who pleaded poverty to the French ambassador NOAILLES after he came with POLE into ENGLAND.
335	GIBERTI bishop of VERONA, did not die " the " year following the prorogation of the first

O 2 TREN-

T. P.

APPENDIX.

"Trentine council" which was on July 6 1543; but in Dec^br the same year,

QUIRINI.

340	Both the translation of the letters, and the reference to them, are false; neither " of his colleagues wrote to him that one LUDOVICO, and an Italian count BONIFACIO, had engaged to seize POLE on the road;" the letter from C. CERVINI from BOLOGNA, p. 284 vol. iv. Quirini, sends him all the intelligence he could pick up of those two persons; but, so far from speaking a syllable about " their lying in wait to seize him on the road," CERVINI rather treats all such apprehensions as frivolous, and hastens his departure from ROME.

The reference is also false; for only seven of the letters say a word on the subject, the 8th and 9th are written the next year, on different occasions.

Vol. 2. PHILLIPS.

p. 6. margin.	Ibid. sex. means, idibus sextilis.

p. 40 margin.	The Pope's answer was to a letter from the queen of the 7th APRIL, not of the 16th.

QUIRINI, p. 435. vol. 4.

44 p.	The translation from the ORATIO DE PACE is strangely blundered.

Latin: Pholio interprete

Meminisse debes CÆSAR! belli hujus initia, quæ quidem non sunt a duorum triumve annorum spatio, quibus Bellum a te cum HENRICO geritur, sed ab triginta aut eo etiam amplius intervallo repetenda, atque tibi cum FRANCISCO hujus ipsius Regis Patre inchoatum certamen.

IV Quirini, 409.

PHILLIPS's

APPENDIX.

PHILLIPS's English Translation.

"The emperor should reflect, not only on the situation of his affairs within these three or four last years he had been at war with the *present king*, but call to remembrance the events of HENRY II. thirty years past or more, since these calamities began, and the almost perpetual state of hostility he had been in with FRANCIS his father."

Here are THREE KINGS mention'd, and HENRY 2d's wars talked of 25 years before he came to the crown of FRANCE, all for want of knowing the common meaning of a little Latin.

The letter from POLE to JULIUS III. unfairly mutilated, where he studiously leaves out Pole's candid confession of the people of ENGLAND's aversion to popery, and the character of A LEGATE FROM ROME sent amongst them; after *alienata a sede apostolicâ voluntas,* follows [in the original, *et inveteratum jam per tot annos, ejus nominis odium.* Quirini, vol. 5. ep. 1.

N. B. The French embassador NOAILLES remark'd this dislike of the generality of the English nation to the appearance of a popish legate, at POLE's public entry, notwithstanding what his foreign biographers glory in to the contrary.

A false translation to save the credit of POLE: PHILLIPS says, he told the king in a letter (to which he refers, p. 52 and 54. vol. v. QUIRINI.) "He *only* considered GARDINER as a *minister* whose loss was irreparable."

But he mis-translates POLE, for, if *he* may speak for himself, he loads GARDINER with the most grofs and shameful flattery, both as a *bishop* and a *minister*.

Hoc tantum dicam, quod jam fensimus, quasi simul cum illo RELIGIO et JUSTITIA laborarent.
p. 52. 5. Quirini.

Having finished my remarks on the unfair and difingenuous ufe T. PHILLIPS has made of C. QUIRINI's collection of POLE's letters and monuments; and the wilful deviations he has made from truth and rectitude; I will clofe thefe strictures with a fpecimen (which I have hitherto purpofely omitted) of his artful difguife, in the unjuft and partial tranflation he has made of thofe infolent and incendiary INSTRUCTIONS given by PAUL III. to POLE, when he fet out on his embafly to the court of TOLEDO; that the vindictive fpirit of that fee; its unremitted refentment againft this nation for withdrawing from *her* ufurped fupremacy; and the perfecuting temper of POLE, the legate on fuch a commiffion, may be fully and fairly difcerned.

Phillips's tranflation of Paul 3d's inftructions to C. Pole. (p. 242. vol. 1. Phillips.)

To lay before his imperial majefty *the whole conduct of the king of England*, in order to prevail with him to ufe his beft endeavours for bringing back his kingdom to a worfhip it *had been conftrained to forfake*, and putting an end to enormities both hateful to God and deftructive of mankind; that he would find a conformity of fentiments in the king of SCOTLAND, and the new Cardinal BEATON: and in conclufion, that all commerce with HENRY fhould be broken off.

He was to reprefent the league againft the TURK, as unfeafonable at that juncture; fince it would
divert

APPENDIX.

divert the attention of the confederate princes *from the more urgent concerns of* ENGLAND, *and of putting a check to the errors of* LUTHER.

That supposing victory afforded them leisure to *concert measures for the relief of* ENGLAND *and* GERMANY, their enemies would be beforehand with them, &c.

A literal translation of the principal part of the above instructions, from the original, publish'd by QUIRINI, vol. ii. Monum. Prælim. p. cclxxviiii.

To lay before the emperor the instructions he has received WITH REGARD TO THE WICKEDNESS AND CRUELTIES OF THE KING OF ENGLAND.

To prevail on his imperial majesty, to bend his whole attention to the bringing back that kingdom to the true religion, and not to suffer the king to brave God, and those SAINTS * WHICH HIMSELF AND KINGDOM HAVE FOR MANY AGES WORSHIPPED, without being chastised for it. That the king of Scotland and Cardinal BEATON WHO HAS GREAT AUTHORITY IN THOSE PARTS, are ready to second him.

That he should therefore forbid all commerce with England, and omit nothing to effect the above purpose.

That, because the expedition he was preparing against the Turks would interfere with THE REDUCTION OF ENGLAND, AND THE EXTIRPATION OF THE LUTHERAN HERESY, he should postpone it.

That even a victory over the Turks would scarce give him an opportunity to take REVENGE UPON THE HERETICS, &c. &c. because &c.

* Meaning THOMAS BECKET.

FALSE

FALSE TRANSLATIONS, &c.

OF

LES AMBASSADES DE NOAILLES.

(A Leyde, 1763.)

T. P.   I Would here felicitate Mr. PHILLIPS on his difcovery of a new book, but that he has been fo unfortunate (tho' I believe I might juftly say unfair) as to falfify his author's words in his very firft quotation.

10
vol. 2.
   "I affure your majefty, if once he comes hither, "he will have the firft place in the queen's con- "fidence, to the no fmall difpleafure of the "chancellor, and of feveral of the nobility, who "on account of their religious principles will "fee, with regret, a churchman at the head of "the miniftry," Phillips, vol. 2. quotation from Les Ambaffades de Noailles, tom 2. p. 136.

Mr. DE NOAILLES could not have written such a falfity to his king; for whether POLE came or no, A CHURCHMAN would be at the head of the miniftry, for GARDINER bishop of WINCHESTER, was then both chancellor, and chief minifter to the queen. But in reality NOAILLES tells his mafter in the letter referr'd to,

"Grands nombres de Millords & du Peuple, voudront mal volontiers porter obeiffance a UN TEL MINISTRE DU PAPE;" that is, A POPISH LEGATE. And he fubjoins the reafon.

"Ayant la dite Dame tant d'ennemis pour la Religion, qu'il faudroit bien peu d'occafions nouvelles pour y voir un grand defordre."   Second

APPENDIX.

Second False Translation.

T. P.
31
vol. 2

So great was the EMPEROR's jealousy of the LEGATE's disapprobation of the Spanish match, that HE prevail'd on Lord PAGET and MASON, to cause one of his (POLE's) domestics, who had been waiting for his lord a month at LOUVAIN, to leave the place.

PHILLIPS's quotation from NOAILLES,
Vol. 2. p. 244.

The passage referred to, is in a letter of instructions to LA MARQUE, which he was to communicate to the king his master. He was to inform his majesty, that the queen of ENGLAND " was re-" solved to marry no ENGLISHMAN, but had " fixed her choice on the PRINCE of SPAIN." In proof of this, he was to tell the KING, among other circumstances, " SHE had ordered letters to be written to MASON (by PAGET, who was not one of the ambassadors at BRUSSELS as Mr. P. has translated it) to desire the EMPEROR to stop C. POLE; and also (which is Mr. PHILLIPS's quotation)

That " THE SAID PAGET AND MASON HAD CAUSED ONE MIQUEL, A SERVANT OF THE CARDINAL'S, TO BE SENT BACK FROM LOUVAIN; not out of any jealousy of the emperor's, but " *pour la crainte & jalousie qu'Ils ont eu de lui,*" viz. the queen's and her servant's jealousy, not the emperor's.

184
n.

Negot. d'Amboise de Noailles. No such book.

100 The

APPENDIX.

T. P.	
100 margin.	The Italian letter of POLE's to the king of FRANCE inserted in the AMBASS. DE NOAILLES was written Dec. 13. not the 30th.
109	The reflexion of the two Mess. DE NOAILLES, is not so much on GARDINER, for governing the QUEEN and her LEGATE, as on them for being govern'd by one *aussi pervers et inconstant*, Ambassde p. 519. vol. 4.
112 m.	The two notes at the bottom of this page are translated from VERTOT's notes to the Amb. de Noailles. vol. 4. p. 344.
115	VERTOT observes (in a note upon this quotation of Phillips's from NOAILLES, where he says, p. 126. vol. 5. Le legat a Sobrement refuse, pour ne se vouloir entremettre des affaires mondaines) That the legate's *real* objection was, "he had been "so ill used by the emperor, that he would not "be concern'd in the ministry."

[203]

PLAGIARISMS

FROM

A Noted *Papistical* Work,

Printed by the King's Printer,

And *published with Allowance*,

In the reign of JAMES II. 1686,

" When (as RAPIN says) monks appeared in their cowls
" at WHITEHALL and ST. JAMES's, and boasted
" they would soon walk in procession through CHEAP-
" SIDE."   RAPIN, anno 1686.

Entitled,

HISTORICAL COLLECTIONS,
&c.

Written by some Insidious Papist,
— The P———ps of his Time.—

PHILLIPS, vol. i.
~~Historical Collections.~~

T. P.
26   THE account of the reception of HEN. VIII.'s book against LUTHER, by LEO X.
             Hist. Collections, p. 5.

55   The queen's speech in court to the king.
             Hist. Col. p. 12, 13.

56 The

APPENDIX.

T. P.

56   The king's speech when she was gone out of the court.
Hift. Coll. p. 14.

Account of the diffolution of abbeys.

165   PHILLIPS.—Hiftorical Collection, p. 26, 27.

PHILLIPS, to avoid too great accuracy, keeps to round numbers.

The HIST. COLL. computes the number of religious houfes fuppreffed at 376. PHILLIPS fays, about 370.

HIST. COLL. values the revenues at 32,000 l.— PHILLIPS, about 30,000.

126   His reflections upon ANNE BOLEYN's behaviour upon the death of Q. CATHERINE.
Hift. Coll. p. 206.

338   The account of GILDS, CHANTRIES, and FRATERNITIES, in particular that of COVENTRY (though he pretends to quote Dugdale, 109, 119) he really took from
Hift. Coll. p. 41, 42.
where is the fame reference.

431   HENRY's laft fpeech to his parliament, for which he quotes Lord HERBERT.
Hift. Coll. p. 61.

432   The feveral farcafms on the dying king; his corpulency; his behaviour to CATH. PARR, &c.
Hift. Coll. 67, &c.

APPENDIX.

All his scurrilous invectives on the reign
Of EDWARD VI.
From the second part of the same
HISTORICAL COLLECTIONS,
Entitled,
A SECOND CHANGE OF RELIGION FOR POLITICAL ENDS.

T. P.

442   His base reflections on the protestant manner of receiving the holy eucharist.
Hist. Coll. 123, 123.

443   The story, of what was said to be written in the register book at PETWORTH.
Hist. Coll. p. 100.

444   The lamentable tale of the building of SOMERSET-HOUSE, which PHILLIPS enlarges upon, has a whole chapter dedicated to it in the Hist. Coll. intituled,

—— Of the sacrileges committed in building SOMERSET-HOUSE—— C. vi. p. 107.

but Phillips, in haste to transcribe, fell into the blunder (Mr. RIDLEY justly ridicules him for, p. 211.) in his quotation; and not seeing the words, THE PROTECTOR WAS BOUGHT OFF OF HIS DESIGN OF BUILDING, &c. he writes, HE BUILT IT on the ruins of the DEANERY and close of WESTMINSTER, of the parish church of the BLESSED VIRGIN, &c.

444 to 446   Are transcribed verbatim from that *infamous* book; nay, even the three quotations referred to in the margin from WHITE, WESTON, and *one* MILES HUBBARD (as that book calls him, p. 126.)

are

APPENDIX.

are not of his own discovering, but are to be found there.

Hist. Coll. from 119 to 126.

The story of CRANMER's sitting on the altar of the Virgin.

Hist. Coll. 109.

The commotions on putting forth the new liturgy.

Hist. Coll. 110.

PHILLIPS, vol. 2.

Historical Collections.

The *ingenious* emark, "that EDWARD VI. died "the same day and month on which HENRY "VIII. put SIR THOMAS MORE to death."

Hist. Coll. p. 143.

Q. MARY's two letters to the council, and the young king, for which he quotes FOX, are to be found, with the same reference to Fox,

Hist. Coll. p. 153. &c.

This is the first place in which Mr. P. takes notice of a book, he might indeed be ashamed to own himself so much obliged to; and he conceals the title of it, even while he is referring to it under the obscure abbreviation of HIST. COLL.

> I must do him the justice to say, his reference is right according to the edition of 1686; in the 225th page of which, this "clear "and solid discourse, so truly comparable "with Tully and Demosthenes," is to be found; though the ARCHBISHOP, who spoke

APPENDIX.

it, acknowleges it to be A VERY RUDE AND PLAIN SPEECH (p. 240.) neither does the harſh metaphor, *twice repeated,* of " LEAPING OUT OF PETER'S SHIP, " AND BEING OVERWHELMED WITH " THE WAVES OF SCHISM," reſemble much the ſtyle either of TULLY or DEMOSTHENES.

T. P.
85, 86, &c.
Mr. PHILLIPS, I am aſſured, has often been ſo weak as to triumph greatly UPON THE ARGUMENTS IN FAVOUR OF HIS OWN CHURCH, SELECTED FROM THE PROTESTANT WRITERS; he has gloried in the diſcovery as being his own, and induſtriouſly pointed out the paſſages, to ſeveral readers of his work who had not met with them before, in Bp. TAYLOR's, GROTIUS's, and HAMMOND's works—He has left them doubled down in bookſellers ſhops, as new objects of triumph to himſelf and his cauſe, and prided himſelf in them as the COUPS DE MAITRE of his whole work.

But behold at laſt!

He is diſcovered to be but a POOR ACCOMPLICE in this mighty offence againſt the proteſtant cauſe; but a MERE *hawker of ſtolen goods,* which he has not ſufficiently diſguiſed to eſcape detection.

For the whole extract from BISHOP TAYLOR (not indeed in the biſhop's own language, but, in what Mr. PHILLIPS has adopted, except the mention of *their miracles,* which he has deſignedly dropt) is to be found in the ſeventh chapter

APPENDIX.

chapter of the APPENDIX to the HISTORICAL COLLECTIONS, p. 387, &c. &c.
Here also is treasured up,
 GROTIUS's first, as well as last, reply to Rivet,
                394
Here are,
The extracts, from Dr. FIELD's preface, 396
     from Dr. HAMMOND on heresy, 397
     from Dr. JACKSON,   398
     from Dr. FERNE,   399
all which he refers to in his note, p. 87.

What Mr. PHILLIPS may merit from graver censurers of his conduct, for thus retailing out the infamous scurrilities of the popish scribblers in 1686, I will not prescribe; but *in the literary world*, he must ever be read and received with the utter contempt and ridicule which is due to A SHAMELESS PLAGIARY.

PLA-

[209]

PLAGIARISMS, &c.

FROM

COLLIER's CHURCH HISTORY, Vol. II.

PHILLIPS, vol. i.

P. 36, to 40, &c. THE progress of the *divorce* is copied almost page by page from this author—The bishop of TARBE's objection—WOLSEY's supposed reasons for promoting it—His persuading LONGLAND the king's confessor—HENRY's letter to the pope—His letter to Sir G. CASSALI — KNIGHT's instructions — The form of the English dispensation— Cardinal PUCCI Sanctorum 4 s. alterations of it — Anne BOLEYN's dislike of WOLSEY from her love to Lord PIERCEY, &c. &c.

119 The account of Bishop FISHER's sufferings (for which he quotes FULLER in the note) he found with the same reference to FULLER.
COLLIER, vol. ii. p. 96.

166 The full account of CROMWEL's VISITATION by his deputies LEIGH, LEYTON, and others.
COLLIER, vol. ii. book ii. p. 104, &c.
Who supplied him with all his references to STOW, Lord HERBERT, and FULLER, in the note below.

213 note. The reference to commissioner GIFFARD's letter to CROMWELL is a false one: the paragraph

P

T. P.	
210	graph in Italics is not in the letter, but is Mr. COLLIER's own remark upon the letter written juft below.
	COLLIER, vol. ii. p. 156.
214 n.	The note of PHILLIPS's concerning the number of mitred abbeys, are the words of
	COLLIER, p. 164.
	Who quotes CAMBDEN, and the FIRST-FRUITS OFFICE.
215 n.	The reference is wrong, though the quotation is right from COLLIER, where are alfo the two references from DUGDALE, and FULLER.
217 n.	The ftory of AUDLEY-END referred to DUGDALE.
	COLLIER, p. 158.
217 & 218	The long quotation from Sir ED. COKE, p. 4. fol. 44. is word for word from COLLIER, who refers to COKE,
	P. 161.
218, &c.	The long reflection upon the ufe of monafteries, and the illegality of, and want of policy in, their fuppreffion, is taken from
	COLLIER, p. 161, &c.
	Thefe being the favourite fentiments of that writer.
222 n.	The ftory of J. BALE's bifhop of OSSORY.
	COLLIER, 166.
264	The ftatute of the SIX ARTICLES 31 Hen. VIII. with the preamble acknowleging the king's fupremacy.
	COLLIER, vol. ii. 168.
290 n.	The bill of attainder againft CROMWEL (tho' he quotes PARLIAMENT ROLLS) he found in COLLIER

APPENDIX. 211

T. P.

      COLLIER, 177, with the affertion, "that he died by a law he himfelf had made;" which Sir EDW. COKE there calls AN ERRONEOUS OPINION; as quoted by

                      COLLIER, 181.

291   The extract from CRANMER's letter in CROMWEL's favour to the king, is from

                      COLLIER, 176.

      Where the whole letter, which Collier calls a "GENEROUS EFFORT TO DISENGAGE HIM," is to be found at length.

292   CROMWEL's dying fpeech is in COLLIER 181, though PHILLIPS chooses to quote HALL's CHRON. and FOX.

293 n.   CROMWEL's character, with the reference PHILLIPS makes to Lord HERBERT and FULLER.

                      COLLIER, 180.

337   The grant of chantries, &c. wrong quoted from COLLIER. The act of the 37th Hen. VIII. is not b. 6. p. 480. but b. 3. p. 207.

339   COLLIER does not fhew, "That PAGET, DENY, and HERBERT, told HENRY VIII.'s executors, that a plan was drawn up for fecularifing the next vacant fees," nor a fyllable to the purpofe for which the paffage is quoted.

            COLLIER, vol. ii. b. 4. p. 219.

APPENDIX.

COLLIER, Part II. book 5.
PHILLIPS, vol. ii.

To Mr. P.'s great convenience, the 5th book of the 2d part of COLLIER's church history tallies with the beginning of his 2d volume, and he avails himself of it, in his usual way, pillaging twenty passages without acknowleging his obligation for more than one.

T. P.
P. 16. Titus, b. 2.
n.
Is PHILLIPS's reference for NORTHUMBERLAND's speech upon the scaffold, which is unintelligible;
The true reference should be,
COLLIER, vol. ii. &c. who quotes it from COTTON LIBRARY, TITUS, b. 2.
But COLLIER should have been fairly quoted, who prefaces the DUKE's speech thus:
"Either *for want of argument*, or *in hopes of pardon*, he was gained over to the ROMAN Catholic persuasion."

38 His account of the queen's commission for depriving the married clergy, for which he refers to
n.
ROT. PARL. 1° Mary, pars 7, he found in COLLIER, vol. ii. p. 364.
Where the reference is also made to the PARLIAMENT ROLLS.

89 His pompous illustration of the ACT OF 1st OF PHIL. & MARY, which he says, "The subject of his history requires he should give the chief heads of," is to be found, not precisely in his words,
COLLIER, vol. ii. p. 375.
But

APPENDIX.

But whoever will compare the two paſſages, and is a little uſed to Mr. P.'s manner of tranſcription, will never doubt from whence he took the ſubſtance of what he has drawn out into six pages.

123 Phillips ſays,
"POLE obtained a warrant from the QUEEN,
"to hold a national ſynod."

The warrant he obtained, was not from the queen ONLY, but from both the KING and QUEEN.

RECORDS, No. 74.

COLLIER, vol. ii.

From which PHILLIPS quotes, in the note, Reginaldi Poli, fol. 6. inſtead of
Regiſtr' Poli, fol. 16.—without any mention of COLLIER from whom he took it, though he has miſtaken in his reference as uſual.

124 to It is more than probable, that he has taken the
140 hiſtory of the national ſynod, and his abſtract of the 12 decrees, from

COLLIER, 388 to 390.
compared with Phillips, 124 to 140.

The preſumption is ſtrengthened by his reference, p. 128. to MS. Coll. C. C. Cant. which is annexed to the ſame paſſage in COLLIER, p. 389.

Though he affects to tell his reader, "He "made uſe of the VENETIAN edition "of ZILETI in 1564."

If ſo, he may lay to that edition, his blunder of calling OTHO and OTTOBONUS, ARCHBISHOPS OF CANTERBURY (for which he has been reprimanded by Mr. RIDLEY, p. 285.) whereas COLLIER, who tells his reader, "He

P 3   "made

APPENDIX.

"made ufe of Cardinal POLE's language," writes,.

> The conftitutions of OTHO and OTTO-BONE AND the archbifhops of CANTERbury. Vol. ii. p. 388.

T. P.

170   SIR JOHN FRESHAM, COLLIER calls, SIR THOMAS TRESHAM.

210 n.   The quotation from COLLIER is unfair (as has been objected) being an incomplete fentence; neither is the reference right, it is in B. 5. not 6.

212   Mr. PHILLIPS muft have been either extremely carelefs, or defignedly hoodwinked, when he was tranfcribing part of COLLIER's 406th page into his character of queen MARY, not to have feen in the collateral column,

> "That the letter POLE indited, fome few days before his death, was not to the QUEEN, but the PRINCESS ELIZABETH, and fent to her by HOLLAND his chaplain, dean of WORCESTER."
> COLLIER, vol. ii. Column 2. p. 406.

167   PHILLIPS's arguments to exculpate the ROMISH church from the odium of the feverities exercifed on thofe fhe calls HERETICS, are not his own, but CARDINAL BARONIUS's, and PHILLIPS found them in

> COLLIER, vol. i. p. 617.

To which Mr. COLLIER (in reply to BARONIUS's fophiftry, thus adopted by PHILLIPS) has given a very manly and fenfible anfwer:

> "Under favour, this endeavour of the CARDINAL's to excufe the ROMAN clergy from "being

"being concerned in the burning of heretics, is but weak and trifling; since when the ORDINARY delivers a HERETIC CONVICT to the secular magistrate, the execution follows as certain as it does from the sentence of a judge when he condemns a malefactor for felony; and therefore to desire *He may be kindly used*, is little better than jest and grimace."

COLLIER, vol. ii. p. 617.

PLAGIARISMS, &c.

FROM

Father PAUL, Messieurs BAYLE, MORERI, and COLLIER's Dictionaries, &c.

T. Phillips, Vol. I.

P. 143, &c. THE whole account of the dignity and office of CARDINAL, which, he tells us in his NOTE, p. 149, is chiefly taken from BELLARMINE and MAIMBOURG, is, beyond all possibility of a doubt to any one who will compare them, transcribed, even to the minutest circumstance, with some fallacious transpositions only, from
> COLLIER's Historical Dictionary, under the word CARDINAL,

Who makes the Reference to Maimbourg, which PHILLIPS adopts.

156 His short history of S. HOSIUS (which he tells us he had from RESCIUS, the writer of his life) he most probably copied from MORERI's dictionary, as he has adopted his blunders, which Monf. BAYLE had rectified before.

Example — HOSIUS took his degrees in civil law at BOLOGNA, not at PADUA (as PHILLIPS says after MORERI)—Neither did he retire to his bishoprick

APPENDIX. 217

bishoprick in POLAND, and finish his works after the conclusion of the council; as they both say—— Mr. BAYLE proves most of his works to have been published before the council broke up:—MORERI and PHILLIPS say, "His works went through more than thirty "editions in his life-time."

T. P. Monf. BAYLE fays, "Il falut y porter quelque "exception."

Bayle fous le mot HOSIUS.

162 Mr. PHILLIPS hath cast rather an UNGRATE-FUL farcafm upon the memory of Mr. POPE (when he drags him in to share in the abufes which he bestows so heavily upon ERASMUS) fince he is obliged to him for fome of the choicest flowers with which he has tricked out the motley style of his history.

EXAMPLES.

Page 63. When intereft calls off all her SNEAKING train.

164 Like AARON's ferpent, fwallow all the reft.

194 Hope SPRINGS ETERNAL in the human breaft.

T. P.
Vol. II. Rejudge his ACTS, and dignify difgrace.
74
POPE.

287 THE CATALOGUE OF CONTARINI'S WORKS
n. (which he fays he collected from the letters be-
Vol. I. tween him and POLE, and from his treatife on JUSTIFICATION) he found in DUPIN's HIST. DU 16me SIECLE, PART I. at the end whereof there is a chronological table of the eccle-fiaftical authors and their works, among which this catalogue is to be found.

318.

APPENDIX.

T. P.
Vol. I.
318-19-20-21.

   The substance of these pages, with the several vouchers referred to in the notes,
    Dr. NEVE has restored to their just proprietor,
     Monf. Bossuet,
      Histoire des Variations, &c.

363 The account of the city of VERONA's erecting a statue to the memory of FRACASTORIUS, and the inscription which Mr. PHILLIPS hath given in the note underneath, he found at length, as he has transcribed it, in his usual common-place book,
   COLLIERS's Dictionary, under the word FRACASTORIUS.

The learned remarks on the INTERIM published by CHARLES V. with those sounding terms of comparison, that make an ordinary reader wonder at the wisdom of the author, are literally translated from
   FATHER PAUL, book iii. sect. 21.

378 " The Catholics compared it to the *Henotic* of
  " ZENON, the *Ecthesis* of HERACLIUS, and
  " the *Type* of CONSTANCE."
        PHILLIPS.

I Literati si ricordavano dell' *Enotico* di ZENONE, dell' *Ecthesi* d'HERACLIO, & del *Typo* di COSTANTE.
        P. PAOLO.

          Had

T. P.
Vol. I. 378

Had Mr. PHILLIPS known of what or whom he was writing, he would have called the laſt emperor CONSTANS, and not CONSTANCE, which is the name of A TOWN, and not of an EMPEROR.

CANONS

CANONS

OF

PLAGIARISM.

1. *THE subtle plagiary will cautiously avoid the least mention of the writer from whom he immediately purloins his materials, but give the names of the remote authors at length, that he may seem to have consulted them.*

EXAMPLE 1.

T. P. passes over C. QUIRINI, and refers to ERASMUS, SADOLET, BERNARDI PINI, SECKENDORF, FRA. PAOLO, COURAYER, &c.

EXAMPLE 2.

He passes by COLLIER, and refers to DUGDALE, FULLER, Sir ED. COKE, PARLIAMENT ROLLS, &c.

APPENDIX.

He will artfully quote the real author for one short paragraph as a subterfuge, after he has palpably transcribed whole pages from him.

EXAMPLE 1.

T. P. quotes four Lines from GRATIANI, and one from DUDITHIUS, when he has transcribed a whole section from the one, and several pages from the other.

EXAMPLE 2.

He quotes the DIATRIBA OF QUIRINI for a single circumstance, when he has translated him page by page for many chapters.

He will either puzzle the inquiry, or tire the patience of curious examiners, by wrong dates, and false references.

EXAMPLE.

T. P. almost in every note, and marginal reference.

UNGRAM-

Ungrammatical and Unintelligible.

> Chartæ nitor, & typorum elegantia, opus hoc commendant, subinde tamen QUÆDAM MINÙS RECTÈ SCRIPTA, & QUÆ SENSUM TURBANT, occurrunt.
> Acta Lipsiensia de QUIRINI opere. Quirini, vol. iii. p. 35.

Specimens of FALSE GRAMMAR, &c.

Preface, p. 11.
 As each of these likenesses is brought within the compass of a few sheets, IT appears to disadvantae.

Vol. i.
12	A candidate OF those arts.
23	HAD BEGAN a correspondence.
40	The services they HAD, and might still, DO, her.
59	Taught them to look on GENIUS and LEARNING as A MEANS.
143	HAS WORE various appearances.
146	It has been the wise POLITY of the court of ROME.
152	We HAVE BORE you.
187	DEFER TO ME—DEFER to his friends judgment.
219	Their disapprobation HAS WENT.
242	Who WAS CHOSE.
261	The eyes of the publick are OFF HIM.
289	HAD BEFEL. 308 HAD BORE, HAVE RAN.

Vol. II.

APPENDIX.

Vol. II.

130   Blemiſhes which GIVE AN EXCLUSION from the miniſtry.
136   Who had INCURRED CRIMINAL CASES.
173   Had ROSE up in arms.
189   He forbade it TO BE BORE before him.
227   He regulated his EXPENCES by the means he had to ſupport IT. &c. &c. &c.

UNINTELLIGIBLE, or rather NONSENSICAL.

Preface, p. viii.

     This DENIAL TRIED by every inſtance of adverſe fortune.

1   His HIGH DESTINY ADORNED with every accompliſhment.
7   Being INITIATED IN A RELISH of this purſuit.
10   In this manner the rays of truth and diſcernment were enkindled, which then enlightened mankind, and ſtill continue to ſhine on it.

     N. B. The next paragraph is ſtill more ſublimely nonſenſical!

11   Sculpture and architecture propoſed thoſe wonderous models of perfection, *to which after times approach in proportion only as they fall leſs ſhort of them.*
12   The HOMEBRED INCITEMENTS determined Reginald.
46   The SUN-SHINE of royal favour ENCOMPASSED him.
94   God has vouchſafed to open the ſacred ſources of truth, in which EVERY THING IS LIQUID AND GENUINE.

114 The

APPENDIX.

114   The two GREATEST LIGHTS were PUT TO DEATH.

123   As long as I had any hopes of ACKNOWLEG-ING IN A MORE PLEASING ARGUMENT.

130   Persuade you to CONFORM TO SUCH UNANIMITY.

271   Whose penitential tears are recorded in such an honourable detail.

Vol. II.

178   The SEVEREST CRUCIBLE is— WHEN those—

179   The following OPPORTUNITY was THE MANNER in which he shewed it.

187   These disadvantages were COUNTERWORKED in CARDINAL POLE.

233   His retreat CONSISTED IN THE OPPORTUNITIES of laying a settled ground-work of that elevation of mind, &c. &c. &c.

These are some of the egregious *solecisms* against *grammar* and *common sense*, with which this author's work (according to his own proper phrase, vol. ii. p. 157) *leopard-like, is spotted all over*.

It would be a very easy task to enlarge their catalogue; but in compliment to my reader's patience, I shall spare for the present any farther enumeration of them.

As to the author himself: THE LITERARY WORLD, who are very placable in their resentments, will perhaps pardon him his manifold offences against them,

In consideration of his resigning up his usurped pretensions to the SCHOLAR, the HISTORIAN, and the ORIGINAL WRITER.

Nay,

APPENDIX.

Nay, even the conſtitution and laws of his country, though attacked by him with unparalleled inſolence that might juſtify a legal inquiry, will look with juſt diſdain on the indiſcreet malice of ſo impotent an adverſary,

———— *Qui telum imbelle ſine ictu Projecit.*————

VIRG.

FINIS.

Errors of the Press.

Page 35, note p, lafciofte, r. lafciaffe.
Pontificii, r. Pontifici.
43, line 2, Sadoleti, r. Sadolet.
45, note, petierent, r. petierunt.
47, line 3, La Mare, r. La Marc.
57, note u, Reûma, r. Revma.
64, n. Italione, r. Italiane.
68, n. h, piegave, r. piegava.
75, n. s, conchavo, r. conclave.
81, n. s, after here, infert mentioned.
83, n. e, Baptifto, r. Baptifta.
85, n. penfarà, r. penferà.
90, n. Bennet, r. Burnet.
92, line 8, wreftling, r. walking.
95, l. 1. after by, add a.
96, n. p. la giunta, r. ba giunta.
della, r. dalla.
01, n. defaites, r. defaite.
02, n. 2, tutta, r. tutte.
112 n. i, attendere, r. attenderà.
118, n. p. He, r. They.
135, n. e, Capifeolia, r. Capifcolia.
144, line 14, dele and.
148, line 3, infert,
At Viterbo alfo he fet at liberty three Italians who were in a plot againft his life.

Check Out More Titles From HardPress Classics Series In this collection we are offering thousands of classic and hard to find books. This series spans a vast array of subjects – so you are bound to find something of interest to enjoy reading and learning about.

Subjects:
Architecture
Art
Biography & Autobiography
Body, Mind &Spirit
Children & Young Adult
Dramas
Education
Fiction
History
Language Arts & Disciplines
Law
Literary Collections
Music
Poetry
Psychology
Science
…and many more.

Visit us at www.hardpress.net

Im The Story
personalised classic books

"Beautiful gift... lovely finish. My Niece loves it, so precious!"

Helen R Brumfieldon

★★★★★

UNIQUE GIFT

FOR KIDS, PARTNERS AND FRIENDS

Timeless books such as:

Kids

Alice in Wonderland · The Jungle Book · The Wonderful Wizard of Oz
Peter and Wendy · Robin Hood · The Prince and The Pauper
The Railway Children · Treasure Island · A Christmas Carol

Adults

Romeo and Juliet · Dracula

- **Highly** Customizable
- **Change** Books Title
- **Replace** Characters Names with yours
- **Upload** Photo for inside page
- **Add** Inscriptions

Visit
Im The Story .com
and order yours today!